MW00585438

GOODBYE, MY TRIBE
AN EVANGELICAL EXODUS

Vic Sizemore

THE UNIVERSITY OF ALABAMA PRESS
Tuscaloosa

The University of Alabama Press
Tuscaloosa, Alabama 35487-0380
uapress.ua.edu

Typeface: Scala Pro, Scala Sans Pro

Cover image: Pew in abandoned church, 2015, Hale
County, Alabama; photo by Allie L. Harper

Cover design: David Nees

Writing that grew into the essays in this collection first appeared in *Appalachian Heritage, Cold Mountain Review, Sol-
stice, Eclectica, BioStories, Atticus Review, Rock & Sling, Superstition Review, Smart Set, Entropy, Port Yonder Press, Humanist, Image*
("Good Letters" blog), *Tiferet, Relief,* and the *Good Men Project.*

Cataloging-in-Publication data is available from the Library of Congress.
ISBN: 978-0-8173-2057-7
E-ISBN: 978-0-8173-9292-5

To Evan, Asher, and Grace

CONTENTS

ACKNOWLEDGMENTS

Huge thanks to the following people: Cathy Warner and Jan Vallone for editing work that grew into the essays in this collection. April Vásquez for keen critical reading. Lys Weiss at Post Hoc Academic Publishing Services for care and attention in working with the manuscript. Joanna Jacobs and Dan Waterman at the University of Alabama Press for dependability and professionalism. Sandra Scofield for being my writing mentor and friend. Most of all, my sister, Alma, for lending a kind ear and wise voice through countless hours of conversation as we both found our way out.

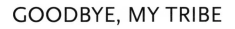

GOODBYE, MY TRIBE

Introduction

Truth and My Tribe

IN THE EARLY HOURS OF November 9, 2016, our Border Collie mutt, Molly Bea, suffered a stroke. She yelped and whimpered in the living room, and I stepped away from the kitchen counter, where I was watching election returns on my computer, to check on her. She crouched in the middle of the floor, frightened and shaky. Molly Bea was a street dog that my wife, Liz, had rescued. She skulked around in fear of everything, would bolt at the sound of a rattling potato chip bag. She feared men most of all. After ten years of Liz's doting care, she still panicked at dinnertime every night, apparently fearing we might yet decide to let her starve.

"What's wrong, girl?" I asked her.

She wagged her tail and stood frozen in her frightened crouch. Our German Spitz, Sergeant Pepper, lay curled into a tiny black ball on Molly's big bed. He raised his head, looked at me for a long instant, and then nuzzled his nose back into his belly with a low grunt. In the kitchen, exclamations crackled out of my computer.

I returned to my barstool and the election returns. Liz and I had left an election party earlier, bewildered at what appeared to be happening. Liz had trudged off to bed in resignation, unsurprised that the country would choose an ignorant lout over an eminently qualified woman. I still refused to believe it, but disbelief morphed into shock and horror as I watched the slow-motion onset of a national calamity.

The following day, when we sent Molly out for her morning pee, we discovered the extent of her damage. She had already lost one eye to a cataract, and now she was completely blind, weak and shaky, unsure on her feet. From then on, we had to walk the yard with her, close beside her, so she wouldn't walk headfirst into trees and lawn furniture. Going out, coming back in, we palmed the side of her head and steered her past doorframes.

Our Virginia neighborhood is the winter home for a flock of black buzzards. Forty or more of them cluster in one tree, on a single house, or in the crisscrossed metalwork of a nearby powerline tower. During the day, they darken the sky over our street in endless circling. They go off to mate when the weather warms up, and return every fall to winter among us. When Liz and I were dating, those buzzards landed on the old Victorian where she lived on the top floor. They dug shingles and tar from the roof with their hooked beaks until rain slid in a thin sheet like a water feature down her dining room wall. Liz discovered federal law prohibits the killing of black buzzards, to the tune of up to a fifteen-hundred-dollar fine and six months in jail—not that we would have killed any of them. We wanted to scare them away, but that can be tricky as well: if a black buzzard feels threatened, it spews vomit at you. Liz tried running around the house blowing an air horn she'd bought at Walmart. The buzzards watched her, unmoving and unimpressed. After Molly's stroke, thirty, maybe forty, buzzards circled silently over our neighbor's house as we helped Molly find her way around the backyard. A few hunched in our white oak tree.

Red, white, and blue Trump/Pence signs flashed by my window as I drove to Bedford the morning after the election. That semester, I was teaching world literature to high school juniors who had tested into early college admission. Most of them were from conservative white evangelical homes in the foothills of the Blue Ridge Mountains: not suburban, but not quite rural, either. They whooped and cheered the Trump victory in the hallways; in the classroom, friendly young smiles beamed at me over Trump T-shirts.

I could not muster the energy to show them how much fun *Don Quixote* could be if they would give it a chance. Poet and singer-songwriter Leonard Cohen had died two days earlier, so I talked about him instead, played some of my favorite songs from his body of work. I ended each class with the song "You Want It Darker," and Cohen's gravelly voice, now not much more than a croak, more spoke than sang the lyrics with the mournful backing of an organ and choir.

Molly Bea was an old dog, had suffered normal age-related maladies, but her aging had been a gently descending plateau. Her stroke was the cliff's edge, after which she hurtled straight for the rocks. We joked that she'd had the stroke upon hearing the election results, and it was true that her plight gave a physical presence inside our house of what was obvious: something had gone awry; with the 2016 election, a trend I had noticed in my tribe for a long time had just come to fruition. My tribe had just inflicted on itself a disaster from which it would never recover. It had plunged off the cliff. When I speak of "my tribe," I am not speaking of Christians generally, but of conservative white evangelical Christians, a sizable subset of the Religious Right.

I felt betrayed by mentors and teachers from my own Baptist youth. I had left their fold—though I still call it "my tribe," I am firmly on the outside of those church walls now—but I continued to hold those teachers in high regard. I believed that, though I disagreed with them about much, they lived their convictions with integrity. I admired them and retained a nostalgic affection for them. Then they lined up in support of a pathological liar, a shameless sexual predator, a willfully ignorant know-it-all, a cruel revenge junkie. They did not slip off this cliff accidentally; they grabbed hands and jumped.

Not long after the election, I asked a couple preachers how they could justify voting for such a man. They rationalized and dissembled, offered me excuses that were astonishingly lame for people who had spent their lives studying and explaining scripture to congregations: they wanted conservative judges; they wanted to make abortion illegal; they wanted to stop the perceived assault on the religious freedom of Christian wedding photographers, cake bakers, and government employees. They turned the discussion toward a catalogue of the ways Hillary Clinton was worse—from her annoying voice and fake smile to the far-right accusations that she had committed drug smuggling, child sex trafficking, treason, and murder. I asked my own parents how they could support such a man, and my mother, in the grip of Alzheimer's disease, still knew enough to say of Hillary, "She's just **evil**."

They justified their choice to vote for Trump by making quips like, "we were electing a president, not a Sunday school teacher." In October 2016, William Galston reported for the Brookings Institution that conservative white evangelicals had changed their tune by "an astounding 42 points." According to Galston, "in 2011, only 30 percent believed that personal immorality was consistent with an ethical performance of official duties. Today, 72 percent of white evangelicals . . . believe that the two can go together."

I wondered how it had come to this. I wondered what had changed. What had happened to those people I respected? How could they plunge hell-bent into something so obviously anti-Christ? What the hell was their faith about, after all?

In 2012, Alice Mattison wrote in *The Writer's Chronicle* that "telling the truth is wrong, if somebody wants to keep it secret." A friend of mine once posted a note on social media that an excerpt from her memoir had infuriated members of her family, and now she was dealing with the fallout at home. Angering family and friends, or hurting someone's feelings, is a perennial concern for most creative writers I know. Another friend of mine recently published an essay about a sensitive family issue with all the names changed and a gender-nonspecific pen name used for herself—or himself, whichever the case may be.

Telling the truth can be a fraught exercise. What I learned from the working-poor people of my childhood in Elkview, West Virginia, was that in your everyday life you practiced stone-jawed stoicism. You did not tell your troubles, and you sure as hell did not air your family's dirty laundry. There was an unspoken code of silence, and it seemed to grow stronger in direct relation to a family's level of dysfunction. Most of the time, anyway.

Sometimes, seemingly out of nowhere, on a Sunday these very same people would come through the church doors and chuck their code of silence under the coat rack with their gloves and galoshes. Standing to testify, they would shamelessly wave their deep personal lives in front of a gathering of neighbors and friends. Even though people listened with interest, there was always the awkward sense that, exciting as the sin they were divulging might have been, an even worse sin—telling family secrets, a thing tantamount to public masturbation—was being committed right there in the sanctuary.

The spectacle always made me squirm in the pew and want to run for the door. It also made me decide to keep mum about my own business. Even now, trying to write about my personal life gives me the heebie-jeebies.

More is at stake than mere discomfort. My friend's complaint about family ire brings to mind a scene from the movie *Henry Fool*. A young man named Simon Grimm is inspired to write. He sits down and pens a long poem, and it rockets him to riches and fame (if you are a poet, the movie requires a mighty suspension of disbelief). We never get a glimpse of what Simon wrote. His mom reads it, though—and she commits suicide.

Why write things others might find hurtful? Doesn't the telling only widen rifts, reopen old wounds? Why rip off those scabs?

Miroslav Volf, in his book *Exclusion and Embrace*, writes that the only route to true healing is first through exclusion—calling out the guilty and naming the sin. Only then can you embrace the guilty one in total forgiveness and love. I must say two things about this: First, I am speaking to my own tribe and am not writing as an injured individual, nor as a member of any group they have sinned against; therefore, I do not stand in a place to offer any kind of forgiveness. Rather, in many cases I have been, at some point, a fellow offender. Second, forgiveness cannot complete itself in embrace without repentance, and restitution where possible, on the part of the guilty. Embrace on the other side of exclusion is far from a given.

When I left the world of fundamentalism, I felt no anger, only the vertigo of having lost my mythology, my paradigm, my Christian weltanschauung. I started writing with the aim of finding understanding. Then, over the past few years, I watched in horror as the men steering my conservative white evangelical tribe sent it lurching from chuckling, good-old-boy white patriarchy toward violent white nationalism. Here in my hometown, Jerry Falwell Jr. bragged in 2015 from his chapel pulpit that he would whip out his pistol—he patted himself where he apparently had a concealed weapon—like John Wayne and "end those Muslims."

I found myself wanting to call out to the true believers I knew who were still at the school, "Stop him! Don't let him do this!" I waited for them to rise up and denounce his violent rhetoric, his anti-Christ white nationalism.

Silence.

As I saw it at the time, conservative white evangelicalism was veering off its true course. Even though I was no longer in the fold, I still believed it was primarily about accepting Jesus as Savior, and then following him as Lord—working out one's salvation by modeling one's life according to his teachings and example. That was how I remembered it, anyway. I had spent my impressionable youth in church pews imbibing the teaching of great heroes of our tribe: Billy Sunday, Harry Ironside, Jack Hyles, Bill Gothard, John R. Rice, Lester Roloff, Vance Havner, Lee Roberson, Bob Jones, Jack Wyrtzen, and Lester Pipkin. Dwight Moody. Charles Spurgeon.

Jerry Falwell Sr.'s Liberty University was the reason I first came to Lynchburg, Virginia, the town where I currently live, the town where my children have grown into young adulthood. Trying to figure out my own history, I had to contend with Liberty University, a bastion of conservative white evangelicalism. I did a lot of reading about the history of Christianity in general and my own conservative tradition specifically.

I read Falwell Sr.'s autobiography *Strength for the Journey* and solid chunks of his jeremiad *Listen, America!* In the beginning of his autobiography, Falwell blames his family's woes on "the Enemy." He is referring to Satan, who was apparently the reason his father was an asshole. In Falwell's public life, however, it becomes clear that he is not so concerned with the Enemy Satan, whom he cannot seem to get a bead on, as with entire groups of actual human beings. He aims his hatred and blame at enemies he sees all around him. People fighting for racial desegregation and civil rights for people of color were his first enemies—the facts of his activism against civil rights are not in the autobiography but are well documented elsewhere. LGBTQ people longing to be free of oppression were the Enemy as well. (Falwell's autobiography was actually ghostwritten by Mel White, a then-closeted gay man who, after coming out, subsequently moved to Lynchburg to live openly and attend Thomas Road Baptist Church with his partner as a protest against Falwell's homophobia.) Women marching for equal rights: Enemy. Big-government liberals trying to force integration, violate states' rights: Enemy. Muslims: Enemy. Communists: Enemy. Anyone else who opposed conservative white evangelicalism. Darwin, Freud, Marx—that unholy trinity that had laid my tribe's mythology to waste. Enemy. Enemy. Enemy.

I began writing these essays before the Trump phenomenon swept across the nation, to explore what happens when your tribe's mythology crumbles beneath their feet. As I wrote, it became clear, at least for me, that the Christianity I had learned was warp and woof with southern bigotry. Looking at the religious leaders of my youth, I found angry blue eyes tight with aggrieved privilege, staring out of the eye-holes in their Jesus masks.

Looking at rank-and-file members of my tribe, I discovered a people just as unmoored as I had been when I left them, in a wild ocean, the heaving storms of a cultural paradigm shift so complete it was washing away everything they held to be gospel truth. They were in a state of panic, grasping for whatever could steady their boats and beat them against the current back into their nostalgic, happy past.

Three caveats: First, I am a creative writer and naturally turn to literature for understanding as much as—more than—I turn to research. I have read and studied conservative white evangelicalism as someone with a deep personal interest. The research I did for these essays was in order to place the narratives of my small-town, fundamentalist rearing within the context of larger American fundamentalism. George Marsden's *Fundamentalism and American Culture* is a foundational work for me, one I have spent a great deal of time with. I do not reference Marsden's book in these essays, but it is fair to say it created the field upon which I interact with all other histories of my tribe. If I get some things wrong, you can assume it is in my misreading of Marsden and not in the quality of his scholarship.

Second, while I did graduate from Liberty Baptist Theological Seminary, I am not a historian, a theologian, or a philosopher. I am a creative writer. That said, I have read both theology and philosophy over the years, at times with staring intensity, as if my own sanity might depend on what I found there. All the same, I am not a scholar. I am a reader and a writer.

As a young man, I briefly dated a girl who had chosen Russian as her major in college. I was an English major, but had not yet taken up Russian literature. Out of sheer curiosity about her love for all things Russian, I grabbed a copy of the first Russian book I came across. It was Fyodor Dostoevsky's *Crime and Punishment*, and with it, Dostoevsky got his hooks in me.

Dostoevsky's epic battle between faith and doubt had a profound influence on my thinking as a young man finding my way out of fundamentalism. I went on a Dostoevsky bender that lasted through his novels and notebooks, to criticism and biographies. This reading eventually spread to Tolstoy, Chekhov, Pasternak. Berdyaev, Kierkegaard, Nietzsche. Unamuno. Camus. Others. Dostoevsky diverted me down a new stream of reading that changed the course of my life every bit as much as war, marriage, and children did. It has led me to this basement room with concrete floor, white-painted cinderblock walls, and silver ductwork above my head. I do my writing down here on a woodgrain kitchen table paint-spattered from my daughter Grace's craft projects.

Finally, the personal stories I tell in these essays are as I remember them. When Mattison wrote that telling the truth is wrong if someone wants you to keep it secret, she was quick to add that "*altering* the truth is lying and we know *that*'s wrong." I know memory is a creative act, and we tend to make small changes to memories every time we bring them up, so the most familiar are furthest from the truth, like a game of telephone inside our heads. Acknowledging that, I attest that these memories are true to the best of my recollection. Without a list, I cannot remember what I'm after in the grocery store, but I have an unusually keen memory of the past—ask my sister, Alma. No doubt, others involved remember them differently, if they remember them at all.

The Rumble of Distant Thunder

ON SEPTEMBER 14, 1966, I was born into a deeply religious and fearful tribe. On April 8 of that year, I had been a translucent fish curling in my mother's warm cocoon when *Time* magazine's black cover read, "Is God Dead?" The *New York Times* had already answered that question the previous January with an unequivocal "God Is Dead"—the headline Elton John sings about in his 1971 song "Levon."

My father was a professor in the insular community of Appalachian Bible Institute (ABI; now Appalachian Bible College, ABC), a tiny fundamentalist Christian school nestled into the jagged mountains of southeastern West Virginia. Since its founding in 1950, ABC's purpose had been to train young preachers and missionaries to go into the world and preach the gospel. Their motto: ". . . because Life is for Service." Mixed with the old revivalist fervor for winning souls was a gentle hippie spirit that had washed all the way up those narrow mountain hollows from the Jesus People wave on the West Coast.

My tribe had no tolerance for long hair, discarded bras, or hippie jeans, but the Jesus People's apocalyptic vision resonated with them: the world was flying apart, Jesus was coming back, and people needed to accept Him as Lord and Savior before it was too late. Outside the gates, enemy tribes warred on all sides. They sang Larry Norman's warning against missing the Rapture, "I Wish We'd All Been Ready," as the shadows of persecution loomed and the sense of foreboding grew dark.

Tribalism developed over the course of millions of years as humans gathered into groups for mutual benefit. They codified the beneficial group behavior into rules and eventually gave those rules warrant from an unassailable authority, an Ultimate Other—a god, or gods. If you followed the rules of your god, you were good with the tribe; if you broke the rules, the tribe punished you, or worse, shunned you, cast you out. When survival depends on remaining within the group, it is easy to believe in the rules. Cast out of the tribe, you wander the moors like Grendel, cursed, despised, vulnerable to enemy tribes.

Though peaceful, my tribe was strict and stern. Members of the tribe watched one another with hawklike suspicion, lest someone flirt with heresy or sin. As the tribe came under attack from the outside world, the standards for proving you belonged grew more stringent, the suspicious side glances at one another over minor points of theology grew longer. Under siege on all sides from various other tribes, my tribe called on our king and bulwark to protect us. Much like a feudal lord, our Lord was the giver of rules, the punisher of transgressions, but He was also the protector—as long as we offered Him proper fealty and homage.

When I was a baby, I lay at my mother's breast under the omniscient gaze of Jesus, our Lord, and I heard the distant thunder: voices talking of events beyond the school walls, the whole world exploding with sin and depravity, signs and omens of the Lord's imminent return. It could happen any day. Wait, watch, and pray. From my earliest years, I heard the repeated admonition to win converts to the tribe. The fields are white unto harvest; people need the Lord; pray without ceasing; preach the Word in season and out. The Lord will not tarry long. Time is running out.

I did not understand any of this, of course, not in the early days, but fear was the atmosphere of my formative years—fear of displeasing the Lord, fear of the Enemy Satan, fear of his minions both demonic and physical, fear of communists, feminists, homosexuals. Fear of war. Armed conflict in Vietnam had already gutted the souls from seventy thousand American carcasses and countless Vietnamese; nevertheless, godless communism thrived even as those corpses festered with rot and flies. The labels *atheist* and *secular humanist* subsumed a wide array of enemy tribes.

Women rose up and established the National Organization for Women to wrest their right of self-determination from men, control their own fertility, and murder their babies. Homosexuals rose up and demanded rights, staged a protest fashioned after civil rights sit-ins, and began fighting back against the police. Black people marched in the streets; a few rose up, called themselves Black Panthers, and took up arms to murder whites and the police. The federal government continued its push to take away the right of states to decide whether to allow mixing of the races. Segregation Academies—private schools where white people could keep their children segregated from black children— popped up in the South. Jerry Falwell opened one in Lynchburg, Virginia, called Lynchburg Christian Academy (now Liberty Christian Academy). Thus, my tribe hunkered down as the culture around them roiled with conflict.

My father was an Independent Fundamentalist Baptist preacher who had trained at ABI, and then at Bob Jones University, where our tribe was bravely holding out against the encroachments of the federal government on racial integration. Elkview Baptist Church in Elkview, West Virginia, called him to its pastorate in 1967. I grew up beside Route 119, a two-lane highway that clings to the loopy banks of the Elk River like the paths of two squirrels chasing—muddy brown water below on the right, jagged mountains above on the left. My immediate neighbors and playmates were the bruised and rowdy children of the Elk River working poor, whose tiny houses clung to mountainsides and the riverbank.

Some of these poor kids would eventually crash cars on those winding roads, a couple would drown in the river itself, and one or two would end up shot dead, but these kids were mostly, to use Ezra Pound's words, the "unkillable infants of the very poor."

The parsonage was painted white, and had three bedrooms. One of the bedrooms was behind another so that my sister, Alma could reach her room only by passing through the bedroom I shared with my brother, Vaughn. Built on a hill, the house was part single-story and part two-story with rooms perched atop a narrow one-car garage. Church bus keys hung just inside the back door of the laundry room. Men in dirty green work pants shoved open the back door without knocking, called hello into the house as they grabbed for keys.

Along the side of the house, erosion had pulled the soil away from the foundation like an old man's gums from his teeth. Where the cinderblocks stepped down with the hillside, an unearthed section of blocks formed the right angle and short sides of a black triangular hole that smelled of cold under-house dust. The receding dirt at bottom shaped the triangle's lumpy hypotenuse. I could wriggle myself through that hole and enter a special secret place under the floorboards.

I discovered the hole only after our family had moved to the big house directly on the other side of the church; the small house then became the church offices. I would shimmy under and find the light switch on the garage wall to the right, and a single bulb hanging from the floor above would blast on. The dirt was so dry that it glowed like the surface of the moon; it was sharp and metallic in my nostrils and sent me into sneezing fits that I suppressed for fear of discovery. Beside the light switch was a half-door made from a piece of wood. I could not open it to the garage, where church mowing and maintenance equipment was stored, because the door was hook-and-eye locked on that side. No matter: what I was there to see—the casket that the church used at Halloween for the haunted barn—was with me there in the crawl space.

Safely hidden under the small white house, I took special pleasure in knowing exactly where Dad was by the footfalls on the floor above me, and the associate pastor, and often Mom too, cranking out bulletins on the army-green mimeograph machine. I also relished the terror of staring at the bright hole I had just wriggled through—by some trick of the light, it looked far too small for a boy's body to fit back out. Every time, it took some minutes to screw up the courage to squeeze my head and right arm through the hole and begin my shimmying out. Still, I went back repeatedly into the powdery dust down there.

I sat in the sharp yellow bulb light and stared at the casket, which looked like it had been made for a poor person: wood covered in gray felt, inside lining of yellowed and stained satin, thin padding. I had memorized loads of scripture by this time in the youth ministry AWANA (Approved Workmen Are Not Ashamed, a reference to Paul's admonition to Timothy in 2 Timothy 2:15: "Study to show thyself approved unto God, a workman that needeth not to be ashamed, rightly dividing the word of truth"). I had a verse for almost every occasion. Here by the casket, for instance. First, "the wages of sin is death," and next, "it is appointed unto man once to die and after this the judgment." Heaven for the saved; eternal burning torment for the unsaved.

My father wore a suit everywhere he went—or, at the very least, a shirt and tie. His leaving the house to preach a funeral was just another thing he did, like church, hospital visitation, and door-to-door witnessing. He had a steady side-gig preaching funerals. I understood that every single day, people up and down that river were falling over dead, going out to meet the Lord and face their judgment—and most of them were going straight to hell.

Staring at the cheap prop poor-person's casket, I thought of Ruthie's dad. Ruthie was younger than I was, a timid girl who suffered incessant teasing from other children at school. Her dad was a drunk with hunched shoulders and toothless puckered face. He drove up and down the river in his decrepit pickup truck asking people for scrap metal. He fawned and backed into himself like an abused dog, overly polite even to us children. His hands were nicked and his fingertips work-blackened.

More than once, after Ruthie's dad lumbered away in his old truck, my father lectured us on the evils of demon drink. Once, I heard Dad say to a church trustee who was there to mow the grass, "It's a wonder he's still alive," and the man agreed that alcohol as a beverage was evil, and used the opportunity to justify his own occasional use of chewing tobacco. Ruthie's dad was going to hell, though, no doubt about it. His miserable life was not even a taste of the torments he would suffer—he was drinking his way straight into the lake of fire.

This was why Dad witnessed to people at the Dairy Queen, why he carried tracts inside his suit coat pocket to give to the man at the gas station, the cashier at the grocery store. This was the Great Commission, truly the one high calling. It had to be an all-consuming mission. What else could even come close in importance?

I stared at the casket under the old house and wondered at the mystery of it all.

For Halloween, churchmen dragged out the casket for a haunted barn. (That was before Elkview Baptist Church threw off the holiday as evil and replaced it with a harvest festival; afterward, kids could still dress up, but as biblical characters, not ghouls.) The barn was at the bottom of our new house's yard, flanked by three apple trees. The "new" house was old, and featured knotty pine walls and a vaulted living room ceiling, which was knotty pine as well. It felt like a lodge. My mother had grown up down in coal country, and she kept a pile of the shiny black stuff piled against the house out back, everything from black dust to rocks as big as my head. Alma, Vaughn, and I carried it in a lopsided coal bucket to the fireplace, where it glowed orange with a heat and intensity mere wood could not reach. Men continued to pop in and out without knocking, now in the actual kitchen and not the side laundry room. They grabbed or replaced van keys, bus keys, and building keys from the rack beside the kitchen door. They offered friendly greetings to us as we stood in pajamas toasting Pop-Tarts or pouring iced tea.

Home and Elkview Baptist Church were like a Venn diagram of two circles so closely overlaid that only a tiny sliver of each existed outside the other. I did not find it odd that there was no boundary between church and home, family and congregation. Religion was my mother's milk, my food, the air I breathed.

What was in that air? We were near the end of the age of grace, and any minute all hell would break loose. Watch and pray, keep your lamps trimmed, the Lord's return was imminent and the end was near.

The myth of our entire worldview was Premillennial Dispensationalism. Developed in the late 1800s by John Nelson Darby, and spread via C. I. Scofield's Reference Bible, whose annotations were, as far as I could tell as a kid, just as authoritative as inerrant scripture. When the first Bibles without Scofield's name on the spine started popping up at church, I began to wonder if that was how heresy would creep in.

This system harmonizes the Bible into an all-encompassing story of the history and purpose of the universe. It is a map, a guide for looking at history, judging present crises, and knowing with certainty what will come in the future. According to Darby's system, the purpose of all creation is God's relationship with humanity, which He carries out according to seven different governing systems, or dispensations:

Innocence: The beginning of human history, this dispensation begins with the literal six-day creation and ends when Eve fucks up, and causes Adam to fuck up as well.

Conscience: Everyone fucks this one up, and God has to drown them like unwanted kittens, except for Noah and his family.

Government: This period is from Noah to the promise that Abraham will father nations.

Promise: This is the period from Abraham to Moses's delivery of the Law.

Law: This dispensation takes us from Moses all the way up to Jesus, and includes the "silent" four hundred or so years between the Old and New Testaments.

Grace: This is the current dispensation, the church age, in which everyone must accept Jesus as Lord and Savior or burn eternally in hell.

Millennial Kingdom: After the Rapture and the seven years of the Great Tribulation, Jesus will set up this utopia for his followers.

Before the first dispensation is eternity past, in which God alone exists outside matter, space, and time; after the thousand-year rule of the Millennial Kingdom is eternity future, in which every person who has ever lived will be fully aware and awake forever, either in heavenly bliss with the Lord or in hellish torment with Satan and his angels.

As a child, I often gazed in awe at graphic charts depicting all of time and eternity. The events leading up to the Rapture—when Christ would hover above the Earth and call true Christians, whose physical bodies would rise from the ground and float away with Him, leaving everyone else to suffer the Great Tribulation—frightened me the most in those days, being on the cusp of it as we believed we were. I hunkered in the church sanctuary watching *A Thief in the Night* (a 1972 evangelical Christian film about the Rapture and the events leading up to it) and begging God to save me—one more time, to be on the safe side—in Jesus's name, so I could escape the evil one-world government and the Great Tribulation that would precede the Second Coming. My father had a worn copy of Hal Lindsey's *The Late Great*

Planet Earth. On the cover, our planet is engulfed in flames. Down Route 119 toward Charleston, Tolley's Bible Book Store had a poster of Jesus hovering above a city, rapturing Christians into the air. Cars below that had been driven by believers are careening and crashing, driverless. A plane is crashing into a building. Christians float away, leaving nonbelievers to their tormented fate. I had to make sure that I was saved and that Jesus would sweep me away in time.

Salvation was not a free pass; our preachers were clear that suffering would come to the remnant of true believers—us—before the Rapture. Civil society would break down and we would suffer persecution at the hands of God-haters and atheists. Although the foretold suffering was frightening, it also caused a heady exhilaration—the time was fast approaching when the Lord would descend from heaven with a shout and trumpet blast, and all our hopes would reveal themselves, vindicate us before the world, and destroy the enemies of God.

The Halloween haunted barn exposed guests to various scenes of torture and death that were very much a part of this physical world, acted out by volunteers in costume. Young preachers waited at the end of the horrors, in a tent where they delivered a fire-and-brimstone message. "You have no guarantee," they preached, "that you will make it home alive tonight. If your soul went out into eternity tonight, where would you spend it?" People accepted Christ, had their names written down in the Lamb's Book of Life. They would not suffer the second death, which was not death at all but eternal torment in the burning flames of hell.

Elk Valley Christian School, up the road at Mount Pleasant Baptist Church, had an entire "haunted island," on Pleasant Island, an actual island in the Elk River across a swinging bridge. It was a better show than Elkview Baptist's haunted barn, so eventually the haunted barn gave way to the harvest festival, and the casket was chucked under the office building, in the dirt behind the square wooden door. It may still be there today.

In 1974, I was in third grade at Elkview Elementary School when what would come to be known as the Kanawha County Schools textbook controversy began. I walked to school every morning, the mud-brown Elk River flowing behind the row of houses to my left; down a short hill from the school playground, it flowed on toward Big Chimney, Mink Shoals, and so to Charleston, West Virginia, where it emptied into the Kanawha River. The textbook controversy eventually flamed into an all-out crisis involving violence, guns, and dynamite. I was in fifth grade when it came to a head. Sunday mornings I stood in Sunday school and sang,

> I may never march in the infantry
> Ride in the cavalry
> Shoot the artillery
> I may never fly o'er the enemy
> But I'm in the Lord's army!
> Yes Sir!

As we belted out the chorus, we marched in place, held imaginary horse reins, and gripped the double handle of invisible .50 caliber machine guns. We shouted the *Yes Sir!* with wide-swinging salutes. We didn't know what the Lord's army was, or how to go about fighting in it, but the adults upstairs in the sanctuary were learning how to join in the fray in what would eventually be called the culture wars.

A preacher's wife on the school board determined that the new textbooks were designed to subvert American and Christian values. Included in the children's books were the writings of people she considered to be secular humanists, communists, and perverts—Allen Ginsberg, Sigmund Freud, Eldridge Cleaver—and one even had an excerpt from *The Autobiography of Malcom X* in which he thanked Allah that he was no longer a "brainwashed black Christian." The preacher's wife started a protest movement, and conservative preachers all over the county jumped to her call.

The school board was not deemed sufficiently responsive, so protest turned to boycott. Coal miners went on strike in solidarity with the boycotters. Members of the Ku Klux Klan rolled into Charleston from all over the state to show their support. Good Christian people would not stand for these textbooks that taught secular humanism and moral relativism. I heard my father discussing the issue with church members. It was on the news. I remember hearing men in the church discuss one example of "situational ethics" included in the disputed textbook, a story that condoned thievery: a man steals an apple to feed his starving son. The refrain I heard repeatedly was some variation of "The ends do not justify the means." You let go of moral absolutes and you've stepped onto the slippery slope to relativism, where anything goes.

The boycott turned violent: gunshots, Molotov cocktails heaved at school buildings. Someone set off a charge of dynamite at an elementary school downtown. Someone tried to set off an explosion at the actual school board meeting, but fortunately it failed. One preacher plotted to blow up two schools but was arrested before he could carry out his plan. The Kanawha County school superintendent closed all county schools so children would be safe while things calmed down. I rode my bike around Elkview, the wind in my face full of freedom and river stink.

In the end, the board adopted the textbooks in spite of the preacher's wife, the miners, the KKK, and clergy with dynamite. Moral relativism, the spawn of secular humanism, had infested the schools, was spreading, and would eventually swallow the very soul of America. In response, preachers all over Kanawha County threw together Christian schools in their church basements. They found teachers among the stay-at-home mothers and a ready student body in those mothers' children. The preachers themselves were most often the de facto principals.

In 1976 my brother, sister, and I left the Kanawha County public schools of Elkview for Elk Valley Christian School. Ironically, it was in the library of the Christian school that I discovered both Allen Ginsberg's "Howl" and, more to my liking at the time, Anthony Burgess's *A Clockwork Orange*. A derelict old house out by Route 119 had been stacked full of donated books and labeled the school library. No one had gone through and looked closely to see what was there, but teachers herded the kids in to find books all the same. I wrote a book report on *Clockwork Orange* in sixth grade, careful to describe the book in ways that did not clue Mrs. Combs in to the actual depths of sin and perversion inside its covers.

Still, our parents believed they had tucked us away from the world of secular humanism, communism, evolution, and situational ethics. We were doing our learning safely in a Christian environment, but enemy factions had arrived in our town, and good white Christians had risen to the challenge, met the enemy with force. Surely they were soldiers in the Lord's army.

Elk Valley Christian School (EVCS) was where I first learned that gays and lesbians were—along with communists, abortionists, and secular humanists—out to destroy our tribe. One day in particular, I learned that the immediate threat was from butch lesbians in downtown Charleston.

I was walking through the sanctuary of Mount Pleasant Baptist Church, with its fluorescent lights in the high ceiling in the shape of a cross, when the pastor stepped out of his office on the left side of the pulpit and called to my friends and me. He was a tall man with a dark brown toupee swept awkwardly across his forehead, just a little too low and a little too dark for the real hair around his ears, and his sudden appearance made my heart skip a beat. My only interaction with authority for the two years I had been at EVCS consisted of trips to Principal Irby King's office to have his "board of education" applied to my "seat of knowledge," as he liked to refer to the ass-whippings he regularly doled out.

Irby King made my friends and me pray to a picture of Jesus, ask forgiveness for whatever we had done that time, and then bend over for a couple of excruciating whacks on the ass. King was proud of his paddle, a board with a handle cut into one end, signed, as I remember it, by boys he had whipped. He spun it in his hand like a tennis racket when he told us boys to bend over and grab our ankles. He once bragged in chapel that he still paddled his two daughters, both grown women but still living under his roof. Even though I was still in grade school, I knew that was perverse in some way; I could see by the stone faces of my older sister and her friends that they knew it, too.

Facing the preacher in the sanctuary, though, I calmed down quickly. The preacher had paddled me only one time, when the principal was out. Though larger, stronger, and much younger than the principal, the preacher was inexperienced at beating boys' asses with boards. He pulled his swing, I assume for fear of actually damaging us, and the paddling barely stung at all.

This morning, he pulled open his light blue suit jacket and showed us the flash of his nunchucks (a martial arts weapon consisting of two sticks linked by a short chain) that he had stashed in the inside pocket, where my own father kept his gospel tracts and breath mints.

"Just in case," the pastor said.

It might seem odd that a preacher in West Virginia in the 1970s would be carrying nunchucks to a rally in Charleston. We were all swinging nunchucks around Elk Valley Christian School at that time. "Karate for Christ" evangelist Mike Crain had just held special meetings at Mount Pleasant, and had spoken in Friday-morning chapel at EVCS. Crain had wowed the students in chapel that morning even before he preached—we had all heard that Crain had accidentally cut Stacie Hopkins's mother's hand while whacking a cucumber out of it with a sword in revival the previous evening. The danger was real.

Crain sold both real wooden nunchucks and plastic practice ones at his merchandise table. Mom would only let me have plastic. I envied the pastor's real wooden weapon, heavy and held together with a silvery chain instead of the black vinyl rope on my plastic imitation.

"In case we have to defend ourselves," the preacher told us.

Seeing that we were still confused, he explained: as a student body, we were about to attend a crusade in Charleston, and word was that radical brute lesbians were planning to protest the event and break up its godly momentum as it made its way across the nation. These were the same radical lesbians, he told us, who were reportedly manhandling protesters at abortion clinics, bullying them as they tried to stop women from murdering their babies.

"These aren't regular gals," the pastor said. "Some of them are 180 pounds or more."

I was in seventh or eighth grade and weighed maybe 120 pounds. I would not have messed with Debbie from across the street, who fit the pastor's description.

Busloads of EVCS students rode across the bridge from Elkview into Pinch, and then we rolled toward Charleston on Route 114, which ran along the Elk River's bank. I was excited as I watched the weeds and trees flash by my bus window. Often Route 119 was visible across the brown river. I wanted to see the preacher battle brute lesbians with his nunchucks—hell, I just wanted to see a real-life brute lesbian!

To my great disappointment, not a single radical lesbian showed up—I suspected they were never even planning to come in the first place, but somebody spread that rumor to get people interested. It was the only reason I was interested. Nobody had the opportunity to spin any nunchucks either. It was the same old thing I was already sick to death of: a choir singing awful songs, a fat preacher talking for what felt like an eternity, and more awful damn songs—the background noise of my entire church-drenched childhood.

The choir wore matching red, white, and blue outfits, and the choir members were young and cute—but they were still a church choir. However, tame squirrels on the manicured lawn of the state capitol scurried right up to people, begging for handouts, something that was far more interesting to us than yet another choir and yet another preacher. My friends and I held out our hands to trick the squirrels into thinking we held nuts and got them to nose right up to our fingers. The day was not a total loss.

As we played with the squirrels, the crusade on the steps echoed out across the capitol lawn. Young and rambunctious, I paid no attention to anything said that day, but nonetheless it was a groundswell. It would help shape my future, would pick me up and carry me years into my adulthood. This had to have been the West Virginia stop of the 1980 "I Love America" crusade. It was a political rally—not an attempt to win souls, not even a call to the faithful to make disciples. It was a jeremiad against the enemies of our tribe, enemies so numerous and whose numbers were still growing, and a call not to turn the other cheek, but to stand up and fight. The preacher who had organized the crusade was Jerry Falwell Sr., and he was there that day to warn us about the dangerous homosexuals and atheists.

I heard a guest speaker in chapel at EVCS tell us that the "God is dead" movement claimed God died of grief because humanity had become so wicked. "I'm here to tell you," he said, "God did not die. God is not dead." God was not only *not* dead, He was alive and well, and that is why we did not need to fear. The choir sang, "Lift up your heads, your redemption draweth nigh," one woman always hitting the high note, but more as a siren wail than a musical note. We would be fine. We would keep to ourselves and wait for Jesus to come to the rescue, as God promised he would. "God said it, I believe it," the saying went, "and that settles it."

On Sunday, March 11, 2012, I lounged on the daybed and read the *New York Times* as the aroma of French-roast coffee filled the den. The obituary section included an article about William Hamilton, the man at the center of the "death of God" controversy back in 1966. Hamilton's ideas had nothing to do with the actual death of a divine being. "The 'death of God' is a metaphor," he told the *Oregonian* in 2007. "We needed to redefine Christianity as a possibility without the presence of God." This was not nearly as radical as it sounded, at least not to academic theologians, who had been dealing with this at the very least since Nietzsche's day.

When the philosopher Friedrich Nietzsche in the 1880s trumpeted the death of God, he was announcing the death not of any god, but of the "metaphysical logos," as the twentieth-century philosopher Martin Heidegger called it in his book on Nietzsche. Nietzsche's point was that God had never existed in the first place; what died was the illusion that we could any longer look beyond the material world to explain our existence in any meaningful way.

The textbook crisis was the wake-up call to my tribe that the barbarians were inside the gates; the crusade in Charleston was our call to take up arms and join the fray. This new preaching was not the gospel of Jesus Christ I was used to hearing. These speeches were about power—how we were losing it and how we had to win it back. For the cause of Christ.

Hamilton wanted to find a path for Christianity in the absence of that bygone conception of God. Doctrinal statements notwithstanding, my tribe did this as well when they abandoned preaching the gospel and took up political activism. Is it possible that the deepest source of their fear was not secularists, modernists, and communists, not women's libbers, Black Panthers, and gays? It seems to me the heart of their fear was a nagging sense that maybe the "death of God" folks were right. Did the leaders of my tribe secretly know what they so vehemently denied—that our mythological roots were dry and dead, leaving our doctrines to shrivel up and blow away?

The fearsome rumble was not the mortar thuds against the outer walls, but the crumbling of the religious ground beneath us, the church walls collapsing inward of their own moribund weight.

The Evidence of Things Not Seen

FROM THE DOOR OF MY childhood home to the front doors of Elkview Baptist Church was a walk of about fifty steps. From the back of the house, step out of the yard and you were standing before the gray, twin doors of a metal pole barn—the church gymnasium. Inside were two sets of basketball hoops on padded poles; the floor markings were not those of a basketball court, however, but of two AWANA circles. In AWANA club, children have team competitions on the circle and learn arts and crafts in classrooms, but that is just a way to get the kids inside the church. The real purpose of AWANA is to make kids memorize Bible verses, imbibe the Absolute Truth they contain, and ultimately ask Jesus into their hearts.

We are in the age of grace, remember; we can only escape hell by asking Jesus to come into our heart and save us from our sin—there is no other way. All these claims are true because the Bible says they are true, and the Bible is the inerrant, infallible Word of God; the Bible is the inerrant Word of God because the claim is written in the Bible, and the Bible is inerrant. Finally, if you question any of these articles of faith, you are at best backsliding, and at worst, not saved and dangling dangerously over eternal hellfire.

This was the constant driving message from my father's pulpit, and the guiding principles of my mother's work as, heeding Paul's instructions in Titus 2:5, "a keeper at home," a housewife. I came to ignore it as best I could—which you had to do to keep from becoming a basket case thinking of all those millions of people dying and tumbling into eternal suffering, all because you had not gotten to them in time with the good news of Jesus. When I was in high school, my chief interests were playing soccer and writing bad poetry to a long series of girls I loved with all the passion in my youthful heart. I went to church every time the doors were open. The soccer team and the Elkview Baptist Church youth group were my circles.

The youth group was vibrant and growing at this time—a cult of personality, as such bursts of activity always are, though parents speak of how the Lord is working or the Spirit is moving among the kids. The "personality" in Elkview Baptist's youth group at this time was Joe.

Joe was one of those youth pastors who seemed to have a sure calling, the kind of guy people described as *on fire for the Lord*. He preached fearlessly, with the zeal of a prophet; unlike others who believed they had the gift of prophecy, Joe did not see it as an excuse to be a loud and judgmental asshole. He was open and honest, transparent about his struggles. It drew us kids to him. He and his wife opened their home to us, were endlessly patient with the teenage noise, hormones, strife.

Joe's Sunday school classroom was packed. He led emotionally charged prayer meetings and revival gatherings, full of crying and repentance. He had a beard and crazy hair, and eyes as wild as those of John Brown when raiding Harper's Ferry.

In 1983, an anti–rock and roll wave swept through our youth group after we bussed downtown to a Marty Tinglehoff crusade. We'd heard how rock music was evil, how missionaries had come back from Africa with accounts of how the beat itself called up demons to possess tribal dancers—the music itself opened a passageway from hell right into the dancer's soul. We liked the music, though, and so far, no one had been demon-possessed from listening to Pat Benatar.

Tinglehoff presented the evils of rock and roll music along with musical demonstrations. He played The Eagles and Led Zeppelin and ELO backward—and, yes, Queen's "Another One Bites the Dust"; play it backward, and you will hear Freddie say quite clearly, a number of times, "It's fun to smoke marijuana"—so that the kids could hear the satanic backmasked messages. After that, Joe instructed us to bring all our secular music cassettes to his house. On his front driveway, on the mountainside across Route 119 from Elkview Baptist, Joe had parked a wheelbarrow, into which we pitched the devil music and hosed it down with lighter fluid. We stood in a circle as the black smoke twisted upward from the melting plastic and coated our nostrils and throats with the taste of chemical poison. Boys took turns squirting lighter fluid to make flare-ups.

I was weak to the power of music, and I caved to temptation. My friend Danny tossed in his cassette of Pink Floyd's *The Wall*, and it fell outside of the blaze and rested there intact. Pink Floyd was my favorite band, and though I felt horrible guilt, I slid the cassette into my pocket when no one was looking. The case was a little melted, but the tape played fine.

Around the burning rock and roll cassettes, we sang songs, and took turns praying. We sang, "It Only Takes a Spark," one from Joe's youth, among other songs. Attempted by a different youth pastor, this could have been a disaster of uncool adult intrusion. Joe had an alternative, though, one that made the adults uneasy, which heightened the appeal for us kids. He had Christian rock.

Offering us an alternative to secular music, he loaded the youth group up and took us to a Petra concert down in Charleston—the same Petra that covered the secular hit "God Gave Rock and Roll to You"—before ersatz rock with sappy Christian lyrics was called "contemporary Christian music."

Joe's approval of rock music—even Christian rock—was a problem. It got the parents watching him. But what got Joe into real trouble with the church leadership was when he questioned the doctrine of biblical inerrancy. In front of the youth group, Joe talked of his intense study of scripture and puzzled over how the Bible could possibly be inerrant—but then backed off and said of course it was. He asked honest questions, and though he always came to acceptable conclusions in front of the class, we could all see he wasn't comfortable with them.

To the church leadership he appeared unpredictable behind the lectern, inconsistent, and doctrinally shaky, and in the end they shunned him. His departure seemed inevitable after the fact, but it was a shock to us when it happened. I never found out if he was asked to step down, or if he quit, but his leaving was abrupt. Disgusted that asking honest questions could get you ostracized, I disengaged from the youth group.

After high school, I worked at the United Parcel Service and did a year at West Virginia State, and then capitulated to my parents' wishes and enrolled at Liberty University in Lynchburg. I chafed under the rules, neglected my studies, played club soccer and lacrosse, and slipped off campus at night to drink beer with friends.

After the spring semester of 1986, I enlisted in the Marine Corps Reserves. Upon my return from boot camp, I enrolled, with my brother, Vaughn, at Marshall University, and moved to the southeastern edge of West Virginia, beside the Ohio River, where it meets both Ohio and Kentucky. I was still not a good student, but I read a lot for the classes that interested me, and I also read widely on my own. In Joseph Campbell's *The Hero with a Thousand Faces*, for example, I read about Osiris, the dying and resurrecting god who was the hope of eternal life for ancient Egyptians, and how their sarcophagi had his face on them because people wanted to literally put off themselves and put on Osiris. The god-man who had beaten death would be their face, so they could get safely through the land of the dead. As I read, I thought of Paul's admonitions in Romans and Galatians to put on Christ, to clothe yourself in him. I also read about Isis, the goddess impregnated by a god—miraculously, as she never found Osiris's penis. She gave birth to a god, just as Mary, mother of Jesus, did.

In my college apartment in Huntington, West Virginia, surrounded by the stink of dirty dishes and my roommate Curt's neglected pit bull, I struggled to fit these readings into my tribe's paradigm. That fall semester, Curt, my brother, and I all huddled around a gas wall heater while snowflakes blew through gaps between the windowpanes. I read *Paradise Lost* for my Milton class. I read his *Areopagitica*.

I still have my Milton textbook, *Complete Poems and Major Prose*, from that class. As I write this, my son is using it for his senior thesis on Milton; I had to reinforce the spine with silver duct tape a couple of days ago. Looking back through it, I see that the young me highlighted *and* underlined the passage in which the sad friends of Truth, "imitating the careful search that Isis made for the mangled body of Osiris," cast about looking for the Truth that has been "hewed . . . into a thousand pieces, and scattered . . . to the four winds."

I read the ancient Sumerian *Epic of Gilgamesh* with its flood story and the story of Utnapishtim, the ur-Noah. Flood stories abound in world mythology, but the Bible's account is especially similar to the story of Utnapishtim. In Genesis, the reason God destroys humanity is that the "wickedness of man was great on the earth, and every imagination of his heart was only evil continually." In some translations of the *Gilgamesh* version, the gods are disturbed by humanity's noise. Excessive noise. What is it about making too much noise that deserves supernatural retribution, whether it comes from gods or devils? You could imagine that whenever large groups of humans are making enough noise to wake up the gods, they are having a very good time or a very bad time, a bacchanal or a war. Excess, then. Too much of something.

Gilgamesh also has a serpent—the enemy and bringer of death—that slithers up and makes off with the magic plant that was to be our hero's shot at eternal life. A goddess creates Gilgamesh's wildman sidekick Enkidu when she scoops up a handful of earth, forms it into the shape of a man, and breathes life into it—exactly as God creates Adam in the Bible. The world of ancient mythology, I found, was chock-full of uncanny parallels to stories I had grown up hearing were the absolute, literal, and authoritative versions of history.

To a child of Christian fundamentalism, this was more than a little disorienting, but those parallels were just the beginning of my trouble. Modern science, as I already knew from the creationism-evolution battle, had chucked all these competing truth claims into the same bin labeled *the best they could do before we knew better.*

Getting out of Elkview, and away from Liberty University, was for me like paddling a canoe from a small creek into a river and onward to the open sea. The mad, stormy swirl of ideas was both terrifying and exhilarating. In contrast, the Premillennial Dispensational theology of my childhood—a Theory of Everything, a universal paradigm—was solid ground, each point taught with the same absolute certainty as every other. I began to notice oddities in this theological landscape. Stones seemed fake, held in place unnaturally—the literal twenty-four-hour, six-day creation six thousand years ago, say; or the doctrine of verbal, plenary biblical inspiration and its subsequent inerrancy—and I started to kick at those stones.

I knocked away one stone, then another. I finally allowed myself to admit I could not believe in a literal talking snake deceiving a historical Eve, any more than I could believe in a literal, historical Pandora. The stone fell away. Then the belief in biblical inerrancy had to go, and so the collapse began. The ground crumbled from beneath me in outward circles like ripples on water. Everything my life was built on fell away until I was floating, totally unmoored, casting about among the twisting and drifting fragments of my childhood faith, trying to cobble together something that I could live with—while simultaneously looking over my shoulder for come-back-to-Jesus talks that my father's preacher friends in Huntington were dropping in to ambush me with.

These developments came with real trepidation. Was everything I'd been taught about the world a lie? Could I voice my opinions and questions at home? Disappoint everyone I knew? Would I become a shunned outsider? Bring the wrath of an angry God down on my head? Would I break my parents' hearts, make them fear for my eternal soul? And what about my eternal soul? Did I even have one? What if I did? What if hell turned out to be real, after all? Would I be betting my eternal destiny on the wrong side of Pascal's wager—betting with my life that God does not exist, rather than living as though He does?

It is no wonder that the tale of the bumpkin going off to college and becoming an angry atheist is a cliché—you have to talk yourself up to leaving, arm yourself against the judgments of your family and community. It is no wonder, either, that so many give up, declare themselves agnostic, and choose to think no more about it but rather turn their attention to actually living in this world.

When T. H. Huxley coined the word *agnostic*, he explained, "It is wrong for a man to say he is certain of the objective truth of a proposition unless he can produce evidence which logically justifies that certainty." To Huxley, metaphysical, religious, and supernatural claims were of no use. People I knew who called themselves agnostic said something like: "No one knows for certain, and there can never be definitive proof one way or the other, so why waste any more time and energy on it?" What can we establish, truthfully, about religion? About God?

Religion stripped of God appears to be what Alain de Botton proposes in his book *Religion for Atheists: A Non-Believer's Guide to the Uses of Religion* (2012). In a 2015 interview on Wisconsin Public Radio, de Botton spoke admiringly of religion, of all the human needs it meets, and said his hope is that atheists can co-opt what is good about it without bringing along its ancient and disproven superstitions.

Next interviewed on the same show was Adam Frank, author of *The Constant Fire: Beyond the Science vs. Religion Debate* (2009). Frank went a step further, saying that not believing in God does not mean he cannot believe in some kind of "spiritual reality," or at least leave open the possibility. He bases this on personal anecdotal evidence: he has had his own epiphanies, and cannot bring himself to admit they are no more than reactions firing off inside his brain. Maybe you say these are soft atheists, not good examples, not real like the so-called New Atheists who take a harder line.

What about the New Atheists? Listen to how they revere science and reason. Go to the *Symphony of Science* website and watch the "Wave of Reason" video. Evolutionary biologist Richard Dawkins speaks of the "new wave of reason, where superstition had a firm hold," his voice auto-tuned to sound like singing. Planetary scientist Carolyn Porco says, "The same spiritual fulfillment that people find in religion can be found in science by coming to know, if you will, the mind of God," as the praise and worship music plays.

I was riding with my daughter, Grace, in the back seat of a friend's car, heading home from a music festival. My wife, Liz, was up front with our friend Virginia, who is weird and fun and loves everything quirky and new. Virginia put on *Here Comes Science*, a They Might Be Giants (TMBG) CD for children. The sing-along melodies and catchy hooks were just what you would expect from the nerd rockers.

Grace, who was thirteen, liked it immediately. Songs like "I Am a Paleontologist" were little lessons about things like the scientific method and what various kinds of scientists do.

Then the song "Science Is Real" came on. They sang that they liked fantasy stories but when they wanted knowledge about the real, physical world, they turned to science. They set up science against religion (and the arts, incidentally) as having a surer claim on reality, on "the facts."

My friend was a product of a conservative Christian home, just as I was—I remember sitting in Sunday school as a child, swinging my feet to the rhythm and belting out, "I'm no kin to the monkey. The monkey's no kin to me. I don't know about your grandpa, but mine didn't swing from a tree"—and we both chuckled a little as TMBG poked fun at some of the beliefs we had left behind.

Then I noticed that at the end of the song, TMBG switched from singing that they look to science for facts to singing that science is where we find truth. With this, they jumped from offering science as a method for trying to understand reality to holding up science as a paradigm of reality itself. The song staked a metaphysical claim for science with confidence born of the eighteenth-century Enlightenment. Science no longer holds that place, and it is not religion that dethroned it, but the very same reason that gave rise to it.

"Science is real" is a claim that cannot be proven by the rules of its own game. TMBG sang, "If somebody says they've figured it out. And they're leaving room for doubt. Come up with a test." But "science is real" is a claim that lies outside the bounds of any empirical test, which is the price of admission into science; using their own rules, they cannot verify their most basic truth claim.

Twentieth-century mathematician Kurt Gödel's incompleteness theorem posits that every system is either incomplete (there are true statements that cannot be contained within it) or has internal inconsistencies or paradoxes (there are coexisting claims that cannot simultaneously be true). A dusty old word from theology class, *antinomy*, refers to assertions that negate one another and yet are still both held to be equally true. It is a better fit when speaking about my tribe, but here I will stick with *paradox*.

We live with mystery, all of us, and we believe paradoxes—not minor glitches, easily overlooked, but those at the place where something major is at stake. Our paradoxes are the load-bearing points, the capstones that hold our structures together.

For Christians, there is, for example, the problem of evil: how, in a world where evil exists, can there be a creator God who is all-good *and* all-powerful? To believe in an omnipotent and omniscient God in a world where evil does not just exist but flourishes, is to cling to paradox. My tribe's favorite theodicy is the free-will argument: God wanted humans to freely choose to love Him, and in order to do that the option of freely choosing not to love Him—to choose evil—had to be real; therefore, the possibility of evil was essential for a moral universe to exist. However, God created the world ex nihilo, and this world contained potential evil (which God Himself well knew would go kinetic with the first two humans he set down in it). That means that one second *before* the creation of the world, when only God existed, potential evil had to exist as well, in some form, in the person of God; therefore, God is not all-good. The essay "The Problem of Job" by the nineteenth-century American philosopher Josiah Royce (which I first encountered in the collection *Religion from Tolstoy to Camus*, edited by Walter Kaufmann) does a good job following various theodicies and showing how they all eventually loop back to paradox.

In the Sanskrit scripture the *Bhagavad Gita*, the warrior Arjuna despairs that if he does his duty and kills his kin in battle, he will bring evil upon himself. He asks Krishna, "How can we know happiness?" which is his heart's desire. Krishna tells him he must do his duty, but "relinquish attachment." He instructs Arjuna that he can achieve his desire for happiness "when he gives up desires in his mind, is content with the self within himself." When Arjuna can act without desire, when for him "suffering and joy are equal," his actions will not affect his happiness. You want your heart's desire, Arjuna? Give up desire, do your duty as a warrior, and you will find it.

Likewise, absolute believers in science make a claim that cannot be subjected to their own empirical method. It is beyond the realm of science. It is a paradoxical truth claim, and they must accept it on faith.

Does it come down to which paradox, which mystery, you can abide? Whether we do it with religion, reason, or science, are we all not trying to sate what the existentialist thinker Albert Camus calls "an appetite for the absolute and for unity"? Is Dostoevsky's Grand Inquisitor right when he says there is "nothing a free [person] is so anxious to do as to find something to worship"?

In a 2010 discussion with astronomer Marcelo Gleiser on the radio show *On Being with Krista Tippett*, writer Marilynne Robinson stated that "contemporary science" is making discoveries "as profound as Galileo ever was, or Copernicus." Robinson marveled at "the idea that we can know things that absolutely revolutionize previous models of the universe we inhabit." This is equally true if we are looking out at the vast universe, or inward at the tiniest structures we have found so far.

Gleiser agreed: "Everything is in transformation at all times." History is a continual rethinking of our myths in light of new discoveries. The enemy is not knowledge. Knowledge, like every other living thing, shifts and evolves. In order to live gracefully with it, we must remain supple and adroit. Gleiser stressed, however, that this does not mean being "pious toward science," because "when you adopt the idea that there is only one way of knowing a thing, then you are robbing humanity of its value."

Robinson went on to say that creation myths "anticipate modern cosmology." They are "the expression of the intuition of cosmology among ancient people." Gleiser agreed: "All the scientific models, the theories that cosmologists used to explain the universe reproduced mythic ideas. There was a universe that was cyclical, like the dancing of Shiva . . . the Big Bang was prefigured by creation myths." For me, it is exhilarating to think of the mythology I learned as a child in these terms. All those stories that were once dead relics come roaring back to life in all their metaphorical (rather than literal) power.

Since the onset of social media, I have reconnected with friends who knew me back when I was a Baptist. They ask me where I stand with respect to the old-time religion. I tell them. In our tradition, there are those who backslide, those who were once on fire for the Lord, who have fallen away, but admit they need to rededicate their lives to the Lord. Then there are those, like me, who have left The Faith altogether.

According to Hebrews 11:1, "faith is the substance of things hoped for, the evidence of things not seen." The evidence of things not seen is faith in those unseen things. This appears to be some very clumsy circular reasoning, and that can be a little frustrating, especially when it demands you disregard anything that contradicts or even questions it. The early twentieth-century Spanish Basque writer Miguel de Unamuno claimed that the longing for immortality in the human soul is enough to justify belief in immortality. Faith itself is evidence that the unseen object of that faith is substantial. Is that all we get? How could that ever be enough?

The absolute claims of my childhood faith, in contrast, offer certainty and comfort in a chaotic and scary world. Even for those who know that the fundamentalists' claims of historical and scientific accuracy are false, the gravity of that world is strong. It took me years of effort to escape its pull, to break free of its orbit. After the first time I left Liberty University, I returned twice, once trying to force myself back into a belief system I no longer bought and once because I needed a job. Most people I know who have gotten free have not done it without relapses.

One of the people I reconnected with via social media was my youth pastor Joe, the one who had been shunned for questioning biblical inerrancy so many years ago. He had been pulled back into the world of fundamentalism, was once again on fire for the Lord. He once again proclaimed the absolute truth of this faith, a truth he knew, as preachers from my childhood often said from the pulpit, "beyond the shadow of a doubt."

There was a time when I felt I had to have all the answers, had to know beyond the shadow of a doubt. No more. I think of a character in the contemporary American writer Don DeLillo's novel *Falling Man*. In the wake of the terrorist attacks of September 11, 2001, she thinks about all the variations of belief in the world and decides she is "free to think and doubt and believe simultaneously." This sounds fair and honest to me.

I do not consider myself agnostic. It is true that when my friends ask, I say I don't know, but it isn't quite that simple. My friend Amy, who is a professor of classics, thought about what we should call someone who doesn't know but hopes someday to find out. She suggested *proupomenognostic*, explaining that *upomeno* means "to await, endure, abide." *Proupomenognostic* sounds right. I await a time when I will know that knowing is possible, even if it is always a knowing that thrives somehow, paradoxically, in the midst of doubt, hunger, longing.

The Holy Fool in Winter

I T IS JUNE 2014, AND Alma, Vaughn, and I have converged on our parents' house to see if the danger is real. Might Dad snap and stab Mom with a kitchen knife? The rain has let up, but the sky is dark and low. From where I sit in the living room, I am looking down Route 119 toward Coonskin Park, which is visible on the other side of the Elk River. The picture window is a gray slab splashed with the blacks and greens of wet trees along the mud-brown river. An occasional car hisses past on the wet road.

It smells like Christmas inside, though it is April. I stopped at a Kroger supermarket on the way in and grabbed two rotisserie chickens—they are heavy on the sage and rosemary today—a pound of roasted red potatoes, and another pound of roasted brussels sprouts. Mom cannot cook anymore, and Dad, as an old-school Baptist preacher, never had cooking as a part of his skill set—except for scrambled eggs now and then. When we visited, he used to yell out through the sleeping house, early in the morning, that he was cooking eggs, as if he were throwing a party.

For the past several years, Alma and I have loaded up supplies and done the holiday cooking here, but even this is petering out. Vaughn has emptied the kitchen of knives sharp enough for easy violence. The chicken is tender enough to tear off the bone with forks. That will have to do.

Two nights ago, Dad called Mom's best friend in the middle of the night and asked her to come quickly—he couldn't stop obsessing over the kitchen knives, and he was afraid he was going to hurt Mom. Understandably, she asked him how she could be sure he wouldn't hurt his wife even if the knives were removed. He assured her he wouldn't. In the end, Vaughn, who still lives within thirty minutes of them, drove over, met the friend in the driveway, and accompanied her inside.

One day later, here we all sit in Mom and Dad's living room. We sit in a circle, as if for Christmas, only without the kids fidgeting to get through Dad's reading of Luke 2 and his mini-sermon before opening gifts. I sit on a dragged-in dining room chair in front of the fireplace. To my right, Mom's best friend leans back on another dining room chair with her ropy, athletic arms crossed. To the right of her, Mom sits on a dining room chair as well. Then Dad, in his blue-gray recliner, and then Vaughn, Alma, and her husband, Mike, squeezed onto the couch below the picture window. The oldest of us, Alma starts the conversation, and eventually tells Dad we are at a loss as to what to do. Is he still obsessing over knives? Vaughn has taken the kitchen knives out of the house, but there are scissors and letter-openers in the house, and Dad's workbench down in the garage is scattered with hazardous tools. If he is going to hurt Mom with something sharp, confiscating the kitchen knives is not going to do much good. Alma asks him for a second time if he actually thought of doing something to Mom with the knives, and if so, what.

Dad has his recliner folded closed and sits on the edge, leaning slightly forward, as if ready to jump up and flee. After a long pause, he says, "No. I just couldn't stop thinking about the knives. I worried that I might start thinking about it."

"So you weren't actually tempted to hurt her?" Vaughn asks.

Dad nods, his eyebrows pinched down like a boy in trouble. He is the center of attention, as usual.

All our lives he was the center of attention, whether at church, or at group meetings, reunions, family gatherings, pool parties. He was always speaking up, and the man stayed on message to the point of obsession, trying to steer the focus of every event or meeting to one single thing: you need Jesus, and if you already have Him, don't forget the rest of the world needs Him, too. Just four months earlier, we sat circled with children and spouses in this very room on these very chairs for Dad's Christmas routine. He tried to lead us in singing "O Little Town of Bethlehem" and "Silent Night," and "It Came upon a Midnight Clear," his strong preacher voice carrying the melody, Mom accompanying him in her clear alto. She enunciated all the correct lyrics—she could no longer remember her grandchildren, but Alzheimer's disease had not yet started corrupting her hymn files.

No one else felt like singing, but the preacher pressed on—he'd had plenty of unresponsive congregations over the years. Plant the seed, and let the Lord take it from there, you can't know what kind of soil your seeds are landing on. After the hymns, Dad read the story of Jesus's birth from Luke 2, all the way to verse 20, where the shepherds all return home, "glorifying and praising God for all the things they had heard and seen, as it was told unto them."

In lieu of the usual mini-sermon, he pulled out a piece of glossy paper snipped from a magazine, and read from it a prose poem–like thing about Jesus designed to convince us that every pursuit in the world, if not done to win people to Jesus, was bullshit.

Remarkably, the poem managed to get all of our professions in—military, law, teaching, economics, writing—so that, but for the glossy magazine page from which he read, he could have penned it himself. He'd made veiled references to my own personal struggles from the pulpit enough in my childhood and youth. I pursed my lips and waited through this part, aimed at me: "He never wrote a book, yet more books have been written about him than any other man in history."

"He can't turn off the preacher," we used to say of our father. That is what he was to us—the preacher—whether he was behind the pulpit or driving downtown to Shoney's Big Boy after Sunday morning church. He spoke in Bible verses and aphorisms, his clear, strong preacher voice carrying to all in the vicinity. As we packed up to leave his house after Christmas, he said, "Thanks for stopping in, folks," as if we were just friendly acquaintances, more members of his congregation. We could easily have said, "Goodbye, Preacher," with a smiling handshake. It would have felt more natural than filing past him and our mother like a receiving line, giving awkward hugs.

During this family meeting to figure out what to do about Dad's knife obsession, Mike sits silently, perusing his tablet. Toward the end, he breaks in and says, "Everything I'm reading says that whatever the focus of the obsession is—knives are not uncommon—that's not the real problem. Something else is causing the anxiety."

We follow this line, ask the preacher what might be the cause. Yes, Mom has Alzheimer's and is in decline; yes, they went to a support group, which, instead of helping, gave Dad a glimpse into his own future as she continues to decline. It scared the living shit out of him. Yes, Mom can no longer run the household—plan meals, shop, cook, wash dishes, do laundry—which she had done as dutifully as any Baptist preacher's wife ever had.

Dad is retired and has plenty of time for these chores, yet the thought of learning all this woman's work fills him with dread. Although he still travels all over to preach, church members have been bringing them meals three times a week as if they are both invalids. He has not been able to preach recently, and this, we discover, is the real problem.

Without a ministry, his life has no value. "I feel useless," he says.

"Isn't taking care of Mom a ministry?" I ask.

"Yes," he says. "I consider it a privilege to minister to your mother in this way." As he says it, his brow stays knit into its deep wrinkles and his eyes do not meet anyone else's.

In his 1984 book, *God, Guilt, and Death: An Existential Phenomenology of Religion*, Merold Westphal examined the believer's ambivalence toward God. Ambivalence begins with the awakening to the "ontological poverty of the believing soul." In short, before the Ultimate Other—God—my existence is worthless. The German Lutheran theologian Rudolf Otto described it as the *mysterium tremendum et fascinans*, the "awful and fascinating mystery."

Westphal writes about two basic human reactions to the experience of an Ultimate Other, in whatever way the Ultimate Other is defined across religious traditions. These reactions he calls *ambivalence* and *resentment*. Though expressed in different ways, these two reactions are universal to religious believers of all faith traditions.

In Westphal's view, I, the believing soul, am drawn to God, to the All, but at the same time, I am repulsed by what this means about the nature of my own existence: when faced with the Ultimate, noncontingent reality, I experience what Westphal calls a "deficiency of being," a realization that my personal existence is small and worthless by comparison. At the same time, God holds out to me the only chance at giving my short and tiny existence any real meaning. Could I be anything but ambivalent? "Like someone standing on the Canadian side of Niagara Falls," Westphal writes, "or a toddler standing before a huge dog, I am simultaneously drawn in and repelled."

"Have Thine own way, Lord," I sang in Sunday school, "Have Thine own way / Thou art the potter, I am the clay." From my earliest years I learned to say, "He must increase, I must decrease," a mantra designed to bring my attitudes into plumb with the already established reality of my nothingness before God.

My tribe described our "ontological poverty" in the direst of terms. My existence is not simply worthless in relation to God, the Ultimate Other, it is also hopelessly dirty and depraved—I am defiled beyond help, a worm in vomit who disgusts the Creator of the universe. My father grew up in a home marked by tragedy, bitterness, and booze. When he and his parents heard of their utter unworthiness before God in the hellfire-and-brimstone sermons of the Brethren Church of Anabaptist Christians, they knew it was true. They understood that, as the eighteenth-century American revivalist Jonathan Edwards preached, "The God that holds you over the pit of hell, much as one holds a spider, or some loathsome insect over the fire, abhors you . . . looks upon you as worthy of nothing else, but to be cast into the fire."

The astonishing part is that sinners in the hands of an angry God are also eternal souls, of infinite value to that same God. In Mark 8:36, Jesus says, "For what shall it profit a man, if he shall gain the whole world, and lose his own soul?" "World" here is the Greek *cosmos*. The implication is that one human soul, since it is eternal, is worth more than the entire cosmos, the whole space/time/matter universe, which is passing away and will end.

Not only are we eternal souls, we have an invitation to help God bring off his eternal plan for the universe. He has a *telos*, an ultimate goal for his creation, and it involves every human who has ever lived. Some in my tribe claimed with French Protestant theologian John Calvin that God chose some for damnation and some for salvation, and others maintained with Calvin's younger contemporary, the Dutch theologian Jacobus Arminius, that every human had the free will to choose heaven or hell. Both factions believed God had a plan for the universe, He was carrying it out, and the only way an individual human existence could have the weight of true existence would be to get in sync with the plan. God offered the opportunity to join with Him in shaping the eternal destiny of other human beings. Eternity is a long time. I heard an analogy many years ago in Sunday school, designed to stress how long the unsaved would burn in hell: "A bird lives on the moon. Every one thousand years this bird comes down to earth and pecks one sand grain from a rock the size of the Empire State Building. It gets one tiny grain and flies with it back to the moon. One thousand years later, it comes and gets another grain. And so on plucking one grain every thousand years. After that bird has moved the whole, massive rock and rendered it a pile of sand on the moon, the time spent would still not be equal to one second of eternity."

If living human beings who die "without Christ" really do burn in excruciating torment for all eternity, nothing could ever be as important as saving a single soul. Nothing. What a sense of purpose, what meaning to life.

My father got a heavy dose of this message at age ten, when his parents accepted Christ and his home transformed from a place of booze and fighting to one of peace and Jesus. Seeing this, he surrendered to Jesus as well, and determined to share this good news far and wide. Preaching the gospel so that, like the Apostle Paul, he "might by all means save some" became his entire life and identity. Out of high school at sixteen, he left home for the newly established Appalachian Bible Institute. That was in 1957 or 1958, and his jaw has been set on this mission ever since. It is not just his calling, but the very substance of his existence, nothing less than his bid for immortality—not as a measure of time, as trusting Jesus gives eternal life, but as a quality of being. His air-hollow, empty being filled up with the heft of God.

When Liz and I announced we would be getting married in the summer of 2008, Dad was not sure he could make the ceremony. He had a preaching gig, and he could not get out of it. It came as a surprise to the woman officiating at our ceremony, but not to me. Close to fifty years earlier, he had missed his own sister's wedding for a preaching gig. Alma, Vaughn, and I have reminisced together about how our childhood was absent Dad-the-father and chock-full of Dad-the-preacher. He passed out tracts, started up conversations with the sole purpose of setting people up for the big ask: "If you were to die right now, do you know beyond the shadow of a doubt . . . ?"

Talking to Mom's friend on the phone—the one Dad had called in the midst of his breakdown—Alma mentioned that we didn't remember him being around much when we were growing up. Plainspoken and brutally honest, Mom's friend said, "You don't have to tell me. I was there while she was home and he was out saving the world."

When he retired in 2006, we assumed he would have a rough transition into retirement. He had only ever been a preacher. But our worries were premature. He found ways to keep preaching. He went on at Appalachian Bible College as "staff evangelist." He traveled all over West Virginia, Virginia, Ohio, and Kentucky, preaching the Word in season and out. He was ever more urgently seeking out preaching gigs. We changed our language about Dad in retirement: it was not so much that he wouldn't know what to do with himself—take up golf, or fly fishing—as that he wouldn't know who he was. We, as his children, predicted an existential crisis for our father when he could no longer preach, so our situation at this moment is not a surprise—only the specifics are disturbing.

Even during this intervention, brought on by his knife-obsessed meltdown, Dad frets that he has already lost one preaching engagement because of this episode, and stresses that he may have to miss another one on Wednesday.

"I don't know what to do," he says.

"The first thing you need to do," Alma says, "is start taking the antidepressants and antianxiety medication your doctor gave you."

"I don't like that stuff," he tells her. "It makes me woozy, and I can't drive." Mom cannot drive him. If he can't drive, he can't preach.

At last we get him to acknowledge that he simply has to take the medication, and that he must see a psychiatrist for an evaluation— not an easy thing to get out of him. He does not want to see anyone who disagrees with his theology. (How can they help him if they do not have spiritual insight, cannot see through to the eternal tragedy—comedy, I guess, if you consider the ending—that has shaped his entire life?)

"This is not about philosophy or theology," Alma says. "They are medical doctors."

After some discussion along these lines, he agrees to do it. From there, we make practical arrangements to keep Mom safe and fed in the meantime. We break up the meeting.

Mom's friend springs up and strides to the kitchen, where she makes a plate of food for Mom. Dad follows and makes himself a plate. I pick at a couple of roasted brussels sprout halves. Garlicky and bright with lemon, they are delicious, and my stomach again cinches in hunger. Mom sits in the dining room eating with her friend. Dad goes down the hallway and returns with his journal, for Alma.

She leafs through it to get an idea of when the obsession started and how concerned we should be. She calls me over and points out a page: along with some Fox News–fueled hand-wringing about Obama and the moral decline of the country are the words, "The fields are white unto harvest." At eighty, he is still crying out in prayer, "Here am I, Lord. Send me."

Hungarian American writer Lawrence Dorr has a fine collection of stories called *A Bearer of Divine Revelation*. In the last story, "The Angel of His Presence," a religious old man takes in his enemy, feeds him, cares for him, does not allow his own people to harm this man, though he is their sworn enemy. The religious old man lives "in total abnegation of the self . . . amidst the running tide of killings and hate, praying for the peace of God for all." He does not just pray for peace for all; he lives it, loves his friends and enemies alike while war rages all around him. He ignores the tribalism and hatred because he sees through his immediate surroundings to a deeper, spiritual reality. He lives his life by this spiritual light. He is a holy fool. The Russian term for this kind of holy fool is *yurodivy*, literally "fool for Christ"; Katerina in Dostoevsky's *The Brothers Karamazov* calls Alyosha a holy fool; Prince Myshkin in *The Idiot* is a holy fool.

Dorr's example is the historical Nicholas of Pskov. Nicholas stood before Ivan the Terrible after the czar had ordered the massacre of thousands of people, the destruction of homes and farms, and the sacking of monasteries. Nicholas castigated Ivan, who could have him killed with no more than a nod, to his face and then, for emphasis, slapped a bloody piece of raw meat into his bare hand.

In the short-lived HBO show *Carnivàle*, in the final episode of the second and final season, Sampson, a little person who runs the carnival, talks to Ben Hawkins, a gifted kid—a holy fool—who is out to stop the evil Brother Justin. Ben is determined to carry out his mission although it is almost certain to kill him.

"What the hell is it with you people?" Sampson asks.

"What do you mean?" Ben says.

"You know what I mean," Sampson says. "You, Jesus, John the Baptist, the whole bunch of you—all fired up to throw your lives away."

It is only throwing your life away if what you believe turns out to be untrue. The holy fool lives by a different reality. I remember reading a story about holy fools who threw rocks at the homes of people they knew to be righteous and left the homes of evildoers alone. It makes no sense until you discover that they saw into a spiritual realm where demons roamed. The evil spirits skulked around the homes of the righteous because they were barred from entering; they were nowhere to be seen at the evil homes because the doors were flung open to them and they were inside. It is all in how you see it—or what you see in the first place.

A few years back, Dad and Mom went to see the movie *Son of God* in an actual movie theater—something that was forbidden in our youth in Elkview. The film so moved Dad that he called me on the phone to describe it. I had read that the movie's Jesus was a sexy European man, with shiny, long brown hair. The Satan character—cut from the movie, but clearly present in the miniseries *The Bible* that preceded it and from which some of the footage in *Son of God* was borrowed—had been made up to be a dead ringer for the despised and feared black president of the United States.

I found that fact alone disgusting, but I was also sure the movie had to be the worst kind of religious kitsch. I listened silently, not wanting to ruin the experience for Dad. He went on to list his health problems for a while, and eventually said, "Keep us in your prayers."

"I'll be thinking about you," I said.

"You need to pray, too," Dad commanded into the phone in his preacher voice.

I waited for the moment to pass so we could move on to other things.

"Are you on speaking terms with the Lord?" he asked.

"That's not a conversation I'm going to have with you," I said.

We waited through an embarrassed silence. We would have been using the same words to talk about vastly different realities—it would have been a pseudo-conversation at best. Dad wrapped things up cordially but abruptly after this. I'm sure he was praying for my soul before he had even set down his phone. I was in danger of hell because I no longer believed essential truths about God and humanity, life and history.

My father is not some outlier in his beliefs. According to a 2015 Gallup poll, 42 percent of Americans believe God created the world in its present form sometime between six and ten thousand years ago; 76 percent of Americans believe the Bible is composed of the actual words of God. Polls by both Gallup and the Pew Research Center have shown that four in ten Americans believe that all humanity is descended, with a sinful nature, from a literal Adam and Eve whom God created full-grown, Adam from dirt, Eve from Adam's rib. Another poll, by Life Way Research, found that 61 percent of Americans believe in a literal burning hell, and 53 percent believe that salvation from that hell comes through believing in Jesus Christ alone.

The real question might be why there aren't more people like Dad, obsessed with saving souls. If you truly believe that people are dying and going to hell—to a burning torment that will last for all eternity—and you believe they must accept Christ as their Lord and Savior to avoid that fate, and Jesus has tasked you with trying to save them, you have two choices: disobey God's command or win souls to Christ. What could possibly be more important than winning souls?

After our family meeting about Dad's knife obsession, each one of us calls him within a few days to encourage him to see a psychiatrist as he promised he would. After a week, I call to see how things are going. The preacher admits that he has not called his doctor about seeing a psychiatrist yet, but promises he will. Instead of seeing a psychiatrist, he sits in his own basement for informal counseling with one of his church deacons—a nice guy, a retired butcher. When we are not satisfied with that, he lines up a few sessions with a licensed counselor—one whose degree is from a Southern Baptist seminary. The counselor tells him he is fine.

A couple of weeks later, Alma calls Dad. The anti-anxiety meds have alleviated his knife obsession, which is good since he is still there at the house with Mom, who is herself doing better on new Alzheimer's medications. Not what we wanted, but it will have to do. Then, several days later, Alma calls me.

"Dad has stopped taking his meds," she tells me.

"Why?" I say. "I thought they were helping."

"They made him woozy," she says. "He couldn't preach." She tells me he is, as we speak on the phone, driving up the Elk River with his guitar, which he uses to lead worshipers in hymns and praise choruses—ladies willing to accompany him on piano are dwindling—in the back seat. Even if no one repents and turns their life over to Christ—since the churches he visits are peopled with oldsters who repented long ago and have been listening to gospel sermons about as long as Dad has been preaching them—he is going to preach the gospel; woe unto him if he does not.

This holy fool will preach until the day he can preach no more. Maybe, when he can preach no more, he will snap, find something sharp, and harm Mom. It is hard to imagine because he has been a gentle, nonviolent man his entire life. Maybe, the day he steps from behind that pulpit for the last time—a day that looms ever closer—the preacher will begin to empty out. Empty, he will wither. Withered, he will dry and crumble. Crumbled, he will blow away and scatter in the breeze. No longer connected by his purpose to the Ultimate Other, he will exist no more and be gone.

Big Bully

W HEN I WAS FIVE YEARS old, an older boy, one of the Elk River
boys, handed me a brown paper bag and told me, "There's
candy in there." We were behind the small, white church parsonage
where my family lived. "I'm not lying," he said. Taking a couple steps
back, he said, "Go ahead. Get some out." Two friends behind him
grinned.

"Throw it down!" my mother yelled from behind me. She slammed
open the screen door and ran down the concrete steps, repeating,
"Throw it down!" she yelled. "Now!"

Confused in all the commotion, I froze and held on to the bag. The
powerful firecracker inside exploded and blew out the bottom of the
bag. I was not hurt, only surprised. The boys fled laughing, out the
dirt road between the pine trees and the Pauleys' flat-roofed house toward the riverbank.

From there, my memory skips to Mom holding up the brown bag
for people and telling them what had happened in serious, pinched
tones, the other women shaking their heads, making proclamations.
The edges of the jagged blast-hole were charred black. (To this day, I
remember who the boy was. Seven years later, when I was twelve, I
would see that same boy wrestle a smaller boy to the ground, strad-
dle his chest, pinning down arms with knees, and slap at the younger
boy's face with his penis. I was in the new parsonage, looking out the
side picture window. They were beside the ballfield that my Mom still
called "the clearing," up by the church's picnic shelter.)

Not long after the firecracker incident, Alma, Vaughn, and I traveled with Mom to a youth camp where Dad was preaching for the
week under picnic shelters and beside nighttime campfires. Though
we were far too young, they sometimes let us join the teen activities. I

lived that week to see my team prevail, whether it was a race, scripture memorization, or a cheering contest.

At the end of the week, as everyone stood in front of their buses to trek back to their home churches, the camp leader called for one more contest: to see which team could run around the camp and gather up the largest pile of garbage. He said on your mark, get set, go, and the teens took off for the last contest. I ran for all I was worth, and found myself at the campfire, where the night before some of the teenagers had thrown sticks into the fire as they took turns crying and turning their lives over to the Lord—two girls had clung to one another as they announced their joint call to the foreign mission field.

There I was the next morning, staring at several boxes filled with ripped-up cardboard and scrap paper. I'd already seen kids snatching up candy wrappers and scraps—a Coke can was considered a good find. All this garbage would win the game, for sure. Visions of being the team hero in the last competition made my spirit soar. Then, fear washed in and cleansed me of any feelings of triumph. Those boxes were probably being saved to kindle the next week's fires, where campers would get saved and surrender their lives to full-time Christian service, and I would fuck it up for them, quench the Holy Spirit—at the time, I knew that if you screwed around with the Holy Spirit, you were treading near the unpardonable sin.

What if, instead of winning me a shower of praise, swiping the boxes got me exposed for the bad boy I was? Freud claims Hamlet's statement that "conscience does make cowards of us all" is as much about one's worthiness to act as it is the justification of the act itself. I wondered if this was wrong in some way I could not understand. (My childhood was filled with *aha* moments in which I realized a new low to my base sinfulness as I endured a good ass whipping, and the possible torments of the afterlife plagued me every bit as much as they did the melancholy Dane.) What if I'm acting in defiance of God's will? What if I am bad—a worthless, sinning worm—and stealing these boxes will be proof for all to see?

Years later, in college, I read Flannery O'Connor's *Wise Blood*, and identified immediately with poor Hazel Motes as he sees Jesus sneaking around, peeking from behind trees, watching Haze everywhere he goes. Jesus was watching me, and I feared being caught in sin more than I feared snakes and bees—snakes and bees hurt, but having a light turned on my sin, especially when I so often committed my sins in utter ignorance of their depravity, exposed me for the worthless worm that I was before God.

I stood immobilized by fear, and heard kids from another team running up the path. They ran past me, whooped and hollered when they found the boxes, gathered them up, and took off down the path. Back at the buses, the camp director heaped praise on those kids, while everyone looked on in envy. My face burned with anger and shame.

During my grade-school years, down the river from Elkview, in Charleston, and on out into the rest of the big, sinful world, the country was falling apart. Jimmy Carter was struggling because Iran was holding fifty-two Americans hostage. Anita Bryant was fighting the good fight against gays who were trying to bully Christians and recruit their children into perversion. The threat of nuclear war with the USSR, and "mutual assured destruction," loomed as dark as Mordor's shadow. In church I heard how secular humanists and atheists and evolutionists, gays and lesbians and abortionists, Hollywood movies, rock and roll music, and virtually everyone and everything else outside the church doors was part of a conspiracy to drive Christians back into the catacombs. The constant message was: be afraid, be very afraid.

I had more immediate concerns. I spent my evenings after school riding my bike and playing in the creek and the river, which in some ways was an idyllic childhood experience. I learned early on to plot my course and keep a wary eye on my surroundings. Every foray from the house was fraught with dull-eyed bullies. I was more or less successful, ran up and down the paved and dirt roads like other boys, sizing up possible threats—which boys I would fight and which boys I must flee. I held my own, for the most part.

When I did not hold my own, I slunk home battered and bruised, and never mentioned a word of it to my parents—it did not seem worth mentioning; it was the price of admission to the world of outdoor play. There was no adult supervision on those riverbanks—Elkview was a

Lord of the Flies world of half-feral boys. Girls did not run those riverbanks at all, and soft boys stayed inside building model cars and watching TV.

Alma, Vaughn, and I were allowed to watch only a few TV shows, as most were tainted with worldliness in some way. We watched *The Waltons* and *Little House on the Prairie*. I loved movies, though we could not go to theaters, either. I relished walking into the church sanctuary to discover the reel-to-reel movie projector set up in the center aisle. It meant a brief dark respite from the endless drone of exhortation, admonition, and upbraiding: three chapel services a week at school, plus Bible class every day, three more services each week at church, plus Sunday school, special meetings, and week-long revivals.

One movie I saw in church was *Sheffey*, about a traveling evangelist. Robert Sheffey was a good evangelist, people got saved when he preached, but I sensed something as I watched. The Sheffey character fit the most common personality type encountered among Independent Baptist preachers and evangelists: the asshole. While my own father did not fit this mold—boorish, loud, pushy, authoritarian—I knew it well.

In one of a very few scenes I still remember, Sheffey is a family's guest, and this woman has cooked him a huge meal on a wood-fired iron stove. He asks her if there are potatoes to go with the meat and she apologizes, tells him no, she failed to make potatoes. He prays over the food and thanks God for it, but comments to God, before saying amen, something like, "Even You know meat is better with potatoes." Everyone laughed at that scene. It was a dick thing to say—she had worked hard to prepare him a meal, was feeding him at no charge. He wasn't just an asshole; he was an asshole and a bully.

Jerry Falwell Sr. preached at Elkview Baptist Church just one time that I recall. I was in junior high school. This time, he didn't have a full choir of students as he had for his crusade on the Capitol steps, he had only a small man who played an electric piano and sang solos—like Dwight L. Moody's sidekick Ira Sankey, who had sung sentimental songs to warm up the congregations before Moody preached, a singing Sancho Panza to Moody's Quixote, a Robin to his Batman.

Falwell's sidekick even had the boy wonder's name, almost: Robbie, Robbie Hiner. He was a grown man, but he didn't look like a grown man. He was not feminine but androgynous, as if he had grown taller but never actually gone through puberty. If I closed my eyes, Hiner's high voice shifted and changed between bluegrass tenor, black woman, and child of indeterminate gender. It was fascinating. Hiner sat down while Falwell preached about the abortionists and homosexuals taking over this once Christian nation, and how he, the preacher, with his college, was going to train champions to go out and battle them and win back this nation for Christ. He had set his sights on a mountain in his hometown that he was convinced God wanted to give him.

After the sermon, Hiner sang for the invitation (a time when the Holy Spirit would woo sinners to walk the aisle, meet the preacher in front, and repent of their sins)—which was normal. What he sang, though, was unusual. No hymn of invitation like "Just As I Am" or "Almost Persuaded," so people could do business with the Lord, get saved or rededicated, which was what happened after every other endless sermon I could remember suffering through. This was an anthem of acquisition:

I want that mountain, it belongs to me!
I want that mountain! I want that mountain!
Where the milk and honey flow, where the grapes of Eshcol grow,
I want that mountain! I want that mountain!
The mountain that the Lord has given me.

Falwell's sidekick had the perfect benediction for this sermon. It worked. My father passed around the plates for a love offering. "He comes with no price tag on his service," Dad always told the congregation when an evangelist came through. "Give as the Lord leads."

After church, people lined up in the vestibule to buy records and tapes. I stood there in the vestibule and listened to adults talk excitedly—Falwell had convinced them that they were in on something big that God was doing. They laughed about how, as Hiner sang, "I want that mountain," his pronunciation of *want* sounded like *won't*. People gave their money. Falwell moved on to ask for money somewhere else. He was going to have that mountain.

Robbie Hiner came back to Elkview Baptist once more. By this time, Falwell had moved on to larger churches with more money to donate. During his concert, Hiner shared a conversation he'd had with a young man about music. He said he had asked the boy what kind of music he liked, and the boy turned on some Bee Gees for him. At this point Hiner played the intro to the Bee Gees' radio hit "Too Much Heaven" on his electric piano, and sang out the first verse with soulful longing.

Hiner stopped playing his electric piano when he came to the word *line*, and he held out the vocal tremolo long enough to get people laughing. I knew the song, even though secular music, particularly rock and roll and disco, was forbidden in our house. Mom would stride in from the kitchen and switch off the TV if we failed to turn the volume down on the K-Tel Records advertisements, and march right back out, leaving us kids sitting there in fuming silence. I was astonished that Hiner had the nerve to play a pop song at all, much less in the church sanctuary.

As he continued singing "Too Much Heaven," he held out the tremolo on *climb*. His naturally high voice did not go into falsetto. An entire row of King-James-Version-only people from nearby Sissonville rose before Hiner had gotten through that one verse, which was the only one he played, and strode indignantly from the sanctuary. Hiner went into a long and awkward explanation. He was only playing it to get to a larger point he was trying to make, and so on. He went back to more southern gospel and Gaither music, and eventually, in trying to air the awkwardness out of the room, started telling stories about his experiences with Falwell himself.

One night before the service, Hiner reported, he had squirted shaving cream into Falwell's suit-coat pockets. After performing his part of the service, he had sat on the stage behind the preacher and waited. Sure enough, Falwell shoved his hand into a pocket at some point. He finished the sermon and the invitation without taking his hand out of the pocket.

That evening after the service, Falwell lunged and grabbed hold of Hiner, wrestled him to the floor, and torqued a painful lesson into

the little man's body. Hiner laughed it off as an example of how Falwell was a regular guy, not a stuffy old pastor type, but I knew what
that was really about. That was big dog making little dog lie on his
back and submit. That was a man who was fine dishing it out—who
bragged about dishing it out—but who was angry and vengeful when
it was his turn to take a spoonful himself. That was the reaction of a
bully, plain and simple.

This did not surprise me, or even interest me much. It fit perfectly
with what I knew of how men dealt with one another. It made sense in
my world, but what I did not understand was that, even though I was
quick and athletic, I was no good at this game.

After two years of college, I joined the Marines, in part to learn how
to fight. It worked to a certain extent—I learned hand-to-hand combat
techniques and gained confidence—but I found the military to be full
of bullies who liked to lord their rank over their inferiors. Maybe it has
to be this way. Big dog intimidates little dog, little dog rolls over, order
is maintained. One gunnery sergeant I had was a large man, a physical intimidator. Once he walked by as I stood in line outside Admin,
and he stopped and punched my arm hard enough to jar my neck.

I hadn't seen it coming. I turned in a flash of anger.

"How you doing, Marine?" he said to me, his smile big and
friendly—he was friendly as long as you did not anger him.

Retaliation was simply not an option, and anyway, it was no more
than a good-natured jab. "Good, Gunny," I said.

He walked on.

Some time ago, I read that several women have now completed
Army Ranger training, and the debate over women in combat continues. I wonder how it will work in this world of men where physical intimidation is an accepted tool of control and promotion. Does it take
a bully to do the job right in the first place? Do countries at war send
their bullies off to meet the bullies of their foes—our blustering Goli-
ath against yours?

As a Marine, I served in the Gulf War. My time in the Marines
was up not long after I returned, and I did not let the door hit me
on the ass. Nobody begged me to re-up; I was plenty strong and athletic, scored high on the rifle range and in PT tests, but I lacked the

inner fight—the willingness to join this world of male egoistic dominance, to buck and shove for my place—and was therefore a mediocre Marine.

In 1998, my first wife, Julie, and I bought a coffee shop/café called The Drowsy Poet and moved, with our son Evan and daughter Asher, back to Lynchburg, Virginia. We ran the coffee shop for a couple of years. Business was good, and we opened a second store in 2000, while Julie was pregnant with our third and last child together, whom we named Grace. Julie and I ran The Drowsy Poet together until we separated in 2003 (we divorced in 2004), and I stayed on at the shop until I sold it and went back to teaching in 2006.

Sometime around 2002, my parents, on one of their visits, took the kids to the Burger King play gym on Timberlake Road for lunch. Falwell Sr. and his wife were there eating burgers while their own grandchildren thumped around in the orange and blue tubes overhead. At some point, up in the plastic tubes of the play gym, Falwell's grandson kicked our five-year-old son, Evan, who came down crying to tell my parents what had happened. They did what people do in these situations, suggested it might have been an accident.

"It was not an accident," Evan assured them. "It was on purpose."

Falwell overheard the conversation, called his grandson (who was not much older than Evan) down from the play gym, and walked him over for a reckoning. Towering over Evan, Falwell leaned down and told Evan that he would give his grandson a whipping right then and there if Evan said it was what he wanted. He asked Evan if that was what he wanted, to stand there and watch this massive man repeatedly slap the boy who had kicked him.

Later that evening, as my father told me this story, he commented approvingly on Falwell's handling of the situation. Maybe, being a Baptist preacher himself, he appreciated Falwell's ability to bully people with their own compassion, twist their arms with their own goodness. This kind of bullying does not need to employ physical intimidation, though in this case it did. Falwell surely intimidated Evan, and then told him he got to choose whether or not the grandson would get a beating with his, Falwell's, big ham hand. Evan could choose to have justice and feel like an asshole, or back down.

Evan shook his head: no, he did not want to see the boy get a beating. After a quick apology, the kid ran happily back off to play. Evan sat with my mother and father waiting to go home.

I had concluded by this time that the elder Falwell was simply a narcissist. He did what he damn well pleased as he built his small empire on the mountain in Lynchburg. The words he used in justification fit nicely into the narrative of trouble he and others were spinning to gather the faithful to the fight and to drum up money. If he turned his bullying toward my tribe's enemies, they were more than happy to overlook his ethical failings and give him their full support.

What's more, they did not just wink at his ethical shortcomings. They appeared to believe, as Raskolnikov puts it in *Crime and Punishment*, that "an 'extraordinary' man [and in conservative white evangelicalism it can only be a man, never a woman] has the right . . . that is not an official right, but an inner right to decide in his own conscience to overstep . . . certain obstacles . . . for the practical fulfilment of his idea." Raskolnikov's extraordinary man—he offers up Napoleon as an example— is very much like our popular misunderstanding of Nietzsche's Übermensch. As different as they are, both Nietzsche's ideal and our understanding of him operate without the restrictions of Christian morality. They reject morality based on a religious tradition and insist on creating their own morality based on its usefulness in achieving their own goals.

Why would any man who actually believes the teachings of Jesus assume the right to "overstep" certain ethical and legal obstacles in pursuit of his own vision? I turn back to Merold Westphal's *God, Guilt, and Death: An Existential Philosophy of Religion* in thinking about the Christian Übermensch. How does a man who believes himself to be above the rules reconcile that with his belief in a God who sets specific and nonnegotiable rules? Remember that, facing our own "ontological poverty" in the face of the Ultimate Other, of God, a believer cannot help but feel ambivalent—both drawn to and repelled by the awesome mystery. The reaction believing souls have in the wake of ambivalence, according to Westphal, is resentment.

This reaction arises because I want to be in control, and I am not, and what's more, the Ultimate Other who is in control is not running the world to my satisfaction. It is not easy for anyone to relinquish control to someone they think is fucking things up. In addition to that, the narcissist cannot abide having second billing in the lights.

I recall countless ministers rolling through Elkview Baptist when I was young, each one leading an evangelistic crusade named after himself, his name and photograph emblazoned on all the promotional material—good examples of resentment in the believing soul. Drivers around Lynchburg for several years sported white, oval window stickers that read NOT I BUT CHRIST. The website printed below the message without intended irony was www.falwell.com. Later stickers changed the website to the church's, www.trbc.com.

Moral bullying is one of the most effective ways to gain power over people. To have a successful ministry, any Baptist preacher must be a moral bully. The key to moral bullying is maintaining control of the categories. This is what enables bullies to come across as gregarious and friendly while at the same time pushing others around. It is easy to strike a magnanimous pose when you are in total control of the game and get to determine the rules.

In another Dostoyevsky novel, *The Brothers Karamozov*, harsh and judgmental Katerina welcomes Grushenka, a fallen woman, into her parlor, heaps praise on her beauty, kisses her hand, "the back of it and the palm see, and here, and here, and here again," making a show of it for poor Alyosha, a holy fool, who reddens in embarrassment. In kissing Grushenka's hand, Katerina, the upright, moral—and financially secure—woman is trying to manipulate the fallen woman into doing her bidding out of a sense of gratitude. "Look how this woman, my moral superior, deigns to kiss my hand," Katerina imagines Grushenka thinking. "She is so kind to stoop to my level. I must try to please her in any way I can."

They could get along so well as long as the tainted Grushenka accepts Katerina's assessment of her and remains in her role of fallen woman. She does not. She asks for Katerina's hand, and then refuses to kiss it, saying, "I simply want you to remember that you kissed my hand and I did not kiss yours." With this, she rejects Katerina's moral categories, and in so doing, any possible control that Katerina, the moral bully, has over her.

What happens when the marginalized and bullied rise up and throw off the oppressor's definitions, demand their own moral vocabulary? Katerina is outraged that anyone could question her opinions of right and wrong. She calls Grushenka an "insolent creature," and when Grushenka remains defiant, she yells, "Get out, you filthy slut! Get out of here!"

If they find their moral categories rejected, thrown off balance, bullies resort to a baser kind of bullying. When Hazel Motes sees Jesus sneaking around, peeking from behind trees, he is not afraid of tender Jesus, meek and mild. I was not afraid of Jesus, either, as a young boy. When I watched, motionless, as the other team grabbed up my winning trash and ran with it down the path, I could have lived with Jesus watching me, but my earliest thoughts of deity were not Haze's sneaky, peeking Jesus. They were God the Father, a giant, stomping ogre, following me around, waiting for the slightest excuse to kick his hard boot into my ass. It didn't matter if what I pursued was sinful or not. If I loved it and lost myself in it, it was taking the place of God in my life, which made it de facto sin—no surprise, sinful worm that I was.

Throughout my childhood, I dedicated, and rededicated, my life to the Lord too many times to count, but it was never enough for God. God was omnipresent, I learned, omniscient, and omnipotent. What I learned also was that He was omni-pissed-off as well, omni-pissed-off at *me*.

In another scene of the movie *Sheffey*, Robert Sheffey takes a woman's husband who is drunk and passed out, puts him in a washtub that he has filled with booze, and sets the tub in the middle of a raging ring of fire. The man awakens and panics because he thinks he is in Hell—he repents of his boozing and gets religion, of course, and all ends well. Recently, my sister shared with me an online meme, a photograph of Jesus, with the caption, "Love me or I'll set you on fire."

It took me forty years to come to this realization: though they seemed at the time to be polar opposites, bullies roamed the church aisles just as they did the muddy banks of the Elk River. When I stood, frozen with fear, at that youth camp as a child, I was not primarily afraid of an ass whipping. I was not afraid of a peeking Jesus. What I feared was that Jesus was going to run and tattle to his dad, the stomping ogre. I was ever in danger of an eternal, burning ass whipping.

No wonder Baptist pulpits are full of moral bullies. No wonder that in the 2016 presidential elections, more than 80 percent of conservative white evangelicals flocked to support an astonishingly arrogant and immoral man, a man who proudly flouted every single instruction of their Lord and Savior Jesus Christ. Scholars are still parsing out all the reasons. Along with white cultural anxiety and racial resentment is the issue of authoritarian personalities: conservative white evangelicals love authoritarians.

That Donald Trump's authoritarian bullying was so familiar to them, even comforting, should come as no surprise. Why would it not? The God they worship is the biggest bully of all.

For Flag and Empire

THE FIRST TIME I REMEMBER Clebe McClary coming to Elkview Baptist Church to preach was on a Cowboy Sunday when I was quite young. Dad had ordered foldout cardboard cowboy hats for everyone to wear. The brown UPS van dropped off boxes full of them, flat and stacked, their strange shape a promise of full, three-dimensional cowboy glory.

A contest complete with prizes had led up to Cowboy Sunday. I do not recall the prizes now, but you won them by wrangling lots of people out to hear McClary preach. I did not participate in the contest. I was young, happy to have the cowboy hat and a Sunday free of interminable classroom lessons.

Clebe McClary was not a cowboy, but he was like one. He had the drawl and the swagger—in my mind, cowboys and army men blended together in western movies, riding horses, slinging guns, getting into fistfights. Killing Indians. Cavalrymen riding to the rescue, the American flag flapping as their high-flying guidon. This was the mid-1970s, a time when the United States was still reeling from the disastrous bloodletting in Vietnam. Robert Self, in his book *All in the Family: The Realignment of American Democracy since the 1960s*, explains that before the Vietnam War, Americans "imagined their soldiers striding the globe as liberty's handmaidens." That image came under intense scrutiny when individual soldiers, and groups like the racially diverse Fort Jackson Eight, openly claimed their right to "think and speak out against an unjust war." They called into question all of our "inherited truths about manhood and patriotism, citizen and state."

On Cowboy Sunday at Elkview Baptist, McClary stood behind the pulpit between the Christian flag and the American flag, displayed equally, where they always stood. I did not question the prominence of the American flag in our Baptist pulpit until many years later. I recited the Pledge of Allegiance every morning at school. Though written by a Baptist minister in 1892, the pledge did not include the words "under God" ("one nation under God") until 1954, when President Eisenhower added them to clarify America's stand on godless communism. As far as I was concerned, the flag and the cross were all part of one whole. The goodness of America and the rightness of Christianity (the Baptist kind) were inseparable.

As a Marine, McClary wore his sharp dress blues and a regulation high-and-tight haircut. A black patch covered one of his eyes, and one hand was a glistening pirate hook—he had been blown all to hell in Vietnam. He strung together anecdotes, aphorisms, and jokes in a folksy southern drawl, and the congregation loved him. He was a hero and a godly man. He unapologetically defended our American version of what Self calls the iconic "stoic, manly soldier," who carried out his duty to "endure and commit violence," in service to his country.

In 1987, Dad asked my brother, Vaughn, my then-brother-in-law, Tom, and me (all of us were Marines) to come to Elkview Baptist in our own dress blues. Clebe McClary was coming back to preach. I think we did a color guard during the service, but I cannot remember for sure. After the service, we stood with McClary over in the gym for proud photographs, while people filed through piling covered-dish lunch fare onto their paper plates.

At Elkview Baptist, full-time Christian service was the single highest calling for a man. But I did not want to be a preacher or missionary so I could not, as my father had, link myself up to the Ultimate Other and find my purpose there. Still, I longed for my life to have the weight of a worthy purpose. This dilemma had eaten at me for a long time, and was probably one reason I struggled to find direction. But serving in the military, protecting people under threat, fighting for those who could not fight for themselves, was a close second to ministry at Elkview Baptist. The unconditional praise from church members validated my decision, the winking pass on my deficient walk with the Lord (for I drank alcohol and committed fornication).

As military men, we strode in their midst as supermen, the ones who defended truth, justice, and the American way.

When Saddam Hussein invaded Kuwait on August 2, 1990, I was camped with my Marine unit in the woods at Cheat Lake, West Virginia, where we were setting 300 pounds of C-4 to blow up a bridge. Four months later, I was camped with my unit off Green Beach, near Subic Bay, Philippines, training for desert warfare in the dense jungle—by Marine Corps logic it makes sense—on our way to Iraq. Those woods were full of locals. We force-marched past homes whose walls were built from our own garbage—heavy cardboard MRE (Meals Ready to Eat) boxes, hammered-flat gas and water cans, cinderblocks, a battered Hummer door with the window glass intact.

One day, as we were making our way with packs and rifles along a trail, a barefoot girl came the other way with a fruit bat the size of a small housecat slung over her shoulder. She smiled at me as we passed.

"She's taking that bat home for dinner," our gunnery sergeant told us. He'd been here before. He'd served in Vietnam.

"They have to eat bats?" a Marine asked.

"They eat better than we do," the gunny said. "They have fruit trees everywhere."

We stopped and set up camp, and locals immediately emerged from the surrounding jungle, carrying bottles of booze, candy bars, knives, whatever they could sell. One Marine said he wanted a cold Coke, and a man ran off into the woods and came back a few minutes later carrying one. He traded it to the Marine for two MREs.

Another Marine sneaked out into the woods with a hooker one night, and upon his return caught hell from Gunny Alford because "these woods are crawling with communist rebels." Gunny told us they were watching our every move. This was before the collapse of the Soviet Union—not long before, but before. Americans were only at the beginning of our transition from the Cold War to the War on Terror; our boogeyman was still Ivan the evil Russian, not yet Ahmed the evil Arab.

This was my first experience of another culture. I was astonished by how little they had, by how resourceful they were—they scrambled and bartered and wheedled what they could get out of us, who had precious little according to standards back home—in their daily struggle to get by.

I spent Christmas of 1990 in that jungle. On Christmas Eve, a helicopter dropped off mail. In it was a box for me with peanut brittle, cookies, beef jerky, letters from home, pictures, a stack of magazines, and a plastic Christmas tree about as tall as an ink pen.

On Christmas Day, we humped to a range, staged our gear, and set two lance corporals to walking fire watch while we sighted-in our rifles. That is where I was when I heard someone shout at the fire watch, who were both standing watching us instead of the gear. Two boys ran out and grabbed what they could and scrambled back into the dense foliage.

I've thought about those kids occasionally over the years, wondered about them. I've wondered about the barefoot girl with the big, bright smile, fruit bat slung over her shoulder. After Mount Pinatubo erupted the next year, in 1991, the United States closed the base at Subic Bay. All the American goods and money coming to the region dried up. What did they do after that? What kind of lives have they had?

As embark Marines on the USS *Tarawa*, our job was to stay out of the sailors' way. But for being smelly and unruly, we were cargo to them, like the jump jets above and the tanks and Hummers below— just as likely to be blown to bits and not loaded back on for the return trip. I hunkered in the hull of the *Tarawa* reading my way through the ship's library. Then we flew off the *Tarawa* and crunched our boots across the rocky sands of Iraq and Saudi Arabia.

In February 1991, I found myself sitting in a bunker under the sands of Iraq, looking through the photographs and letters of an Iraqi soldier who lay stiff with rigor mortis above me, 20 feet from his severed arm. Looking through his personal belongings like a ghoul, I found letters, a book, a razor and brush, toothpaste. A photograph of a handsome young man in uniform—no telling if it was the dead man himself or someone else—for all I know it could have been the man he loved.

The sense swept over me that the dead Iraqi above was like me in more essential ways than he was not. Here was the evidence of his hopes and dreams, and they had nothing to do with *jihad* as Americans understood it. He was just a guy stuck out in the miserable desert waiting to meet the coming enemy and fight, afraid for his life. I was ashamed of my part in his death.

Jesus teaches his disciples that, although they have been taught to love their neighbors and hate their enemies, he commands them to love their enemies. Faced with the undeniable humanity of the Other, this is not as hard to do as you might think. I felt a strange affection for the dead Iraqi soldier whom I did not know.

In a powerful scene in Erich Maria Remarque's World War I novel *All Quiet on the Western Front*, the protagonist Paul looks at his enemies, Russian prisoners, and thinks how things would be different "if I could know more of them, what their names are, how they live, what they are waiting for, what their burdens are." He concludes, "A word of command has made these silent figures our enemies; a word of command might transform them into our friends."

In another scene, pinned down in a foxhole with an enemy soldier he has stabbed, Paul waits for the man to die, unable to bring himself to finish the job. The man's lungs gurgle as Paul waits for a lull in the fighting to make his break. When the man finally dies, Paul addresses him: "But now, for the first time, I see you are a man like me. I thought of your hand-grenades, of your bayonet, of your rifle; now I see your wife, and your face and our fellowship . . . Why do they never tell us that you are poor devils like us, that your mothers are just as anxious as ours, and that we have the same fear of dying and the same agony—forgive me, comrade; how could you be my enemy? If we threw away these rifles and this uniform you could be my brother."

During the famous Christmas Truce of 1914, German and British troops did act as brothers. They laid down their weapons and celebrated Christmas together in the no man's land between them. The trench lines were so close in places that the soldiers could converse with one another during hostilities, while they were supposed to be killing one another. A British soldier named Murdoch Wood later said of that time, "If we had been left to ourselves there would never have been another shot fired."

Recoiling from the murder of another human is the first natural reaction to combat. It is every bit as strong as the desire to stay alive oneself. We see the great Pandava warrior Arjuna having just such a crisis in the *Bhagavad Gita*. Krishna drives his chariot in the no man's land between sides. Arjuna sees people he recognizes over there, members of his extended family. He cries out, "It is not good, O Keshav! nought of good / Can spring from mutual slaughter!"

I did not realize it then, but what I felt for the slain Iraqi was grief. I had a small shortwave radio that Joe, my youth pastor from Elkview, had sent me, but I still could not get much news. I certainly could not take part in the TV parties going on back home, watching and cheering as these amazing new smart bombs zeroed in on their targets, blew right through a building's front door with lethal precision. I saw actual humans who were killed—it is not marvelous, not something to wonder and smile at like fireworks on the Fourth of July. Looking down at those board-stiff corpses, I felt no sense of triumph over those dead men; I felt deep sadness.

I felt something else as well—or sensed it—something that had taken hold of me when we were tromping through the forest off Green Beach in the Philippines. It was a growing uneasiness with what we, the US military, were doing in the world. I saw that we strode among the restaurants, bars, and massage parlors of Olongapo City as lords, while the locals simpered and bowed, and held out jewelry, watches, and grilled meat for sale—I could not help but think they had to resent us, had to nurse a deep hatred. I did not understand it at the time, but this relationship had a history of several hundred years.

Vinnie Rotondaro writes for the *National Catholic Reporter* that "in 1452, the papal bull *Dum Diversas* instructed the Portuguese crown 'to invade, capture, vanquish, and subdue all Saracens, pagans, and other enemies of Christ, to put them into perpetual slavery, and to take away all their possessions and property.'" More bulls followed, and they gave Christian European nations carte blanche to explore and colonize the world, to slaughter and enslave non-Christian populations, and to steal their land and its resources.

The United States wrested the Philippines from Spain in 1899, and our military quashed a revolt by Philippine forces attempting to shrug off imperial rule, which the United States allowed fully in 1946 after ending the Japanese occupation of the islands. We did not leave, of course. Our naval base at Subic was the hub around which the local economy churned.

We were a nation created by imperial powers and now an empire in our own right—*the* empire, since the Soviet Union was falling apart—and we were on our way to Iraq. In Iraq's war with Iran, Saddam Hussein had served the interests of America. Then he had misunderstood our diplomat. When she said the United States was not particularly interested in his border dispute with Kuwait, he thought we had given him the green light to invade. He was wrong, and the most powerful army in the history of the world was coming to punish him. He put a brave face on it, but the US military ran his troops out of Kuwait like a grown man shooing a child from his backyard.

We were not just a powerful empire, though. We were the defenders of Kuwait, the little guy who'd been overrun by a bully. We were Superman, clean and white and on the side of truth and justice, coming to give the bully what for and set the bullied victim back on his feet. We were a Christian nation, doing the will of God.

Twelve years later, President George W. Bush sent our forces back into Iraq. In his 2003 State of the Union address, he called on the God "behind all of life, and all of history," and said, "We go forward with confidence, because this call of history has come to the right country. May He guide us now." Bush, in his cowboy hat and cowboy boots. Bush, the gun-slinging American.

Our troops rolled through Iraq without so much as a speed bump, shocked and awed the enemy. Iraqi forces crumbled before US might. We strafed soldiers and civilians alike as they fled. Living humans who, like us, had hearts full of dreams and fears, were reduced to inanimate clumps of rotting flesh. I sat in my living room in the evenings while Julie worked at our coffee shop and our children slept peacefully down the hallway. I stared at the continual stream of war footage and commentary on TV. I cannot say now what I felt. I don't remember. I know it was not pride.

A March 2015 report from Physicians for Social Responsibility titled *Body Count* revealed that President Bush's God-ordained "war on terror" had at that time left 1 million dead in Iraq (5 percent of the total population of the country), 220,000 dead in Afghanistan, and 80,000 dead in Pakistan—numbers tantamount to genocide.

The Doctrine of Discovery—and white supremacy—lies at the root of Manifest Destiny, the nineteenth-century declaration that it was God's providential purpose for white Americans to spread their rule westward all the way to the Pacific Ocean. The editor's note attached to Rotondaro's essay in the *National Catholic Reporter* explains, "It may seem like papal statements from 500 years ago are ancient history. But Native American activists and scholars insist that Catholicism's past continues to affect the present. Papal bulls from the 1400s condoned the conquest of the Americas and other lands inhabited by indigenous people. The papal documents led to an international norm called the Doctrine of Discovery, which dehumanized non-Christians and legitimized their suppression by nations around the world, including by the United States."

Rotondaro reveals that as recently as 2005, the Doctrine of Discovery was referenced in a Supreme Court decision against Native American property claims. "The decision," Rotondaro tells us, "precluded 'the tribe from rekindling embers of sovereignty that long ago grew cold,' Justice Ruth Bader Ginsburg wrote for the majority."

It seems to me that understanding the Doctrine of Discovery, and its assumption of Christian, European supremacy, is essential to understanding US military involvement in the world yet today. It is essential to understanding current Native American land disputes and protests. It is essential to understanding race relations. In the oft-quoted words of William Faulkner, "The past is never dead. It's not even past."

In the summer of 2016, my wife, Liz, and I tried out a new brewery down the road from us in Bedford, Virginia. It is in a restored factory building with brick walls and high ceilings. Beside the bar, a floor-to-ceiling glass wall reveals the brewing floor—equipment and hoses on carts, boilers, cone-bottomed fermentation tanks. We drank a flight of their beers and dined on barbecue and home-fried pork rinds as echoing chatter drowned out southern fried rock and roll.

I glanced up and noticed, among the western-themed decor, a huge US flag hanging on the wall to the right of the entrance. Big as an apartment patio, the flag, once I registered its presence, never faded back into the scenery. It dominated the room, and I found I did not like it. As a veteran of Desert Shield/Desert Storm, I once viewed the flag with simple, chest-swelling pride. That night I was ambivalent. I fear that to most of the people drinking there around me that night—Bedford is deep in Donald Trump country—that flag represented an America they clung to as fervently as I wanted to see it pass away.

My ambivalence intensified on Veterans Day when I awoke to find a flag smaller than a sheet of notebook paper shoved into the ground beside my mailbox. Looking up and down the street, I saw that all my neighbors had them, too. I walked down the driveway to discover a tag on the flag stick with the name of my member of Congress printed on it.

This politician's positions were consistently against social and racial justice and for white exclusivism, and they were odious to me. Finding a flag planted in my front yard with his name attached to it was disgusting—just as seeing white nationalists waving American flags alongside Nazi and Confederate flags in Charlottesville several months later was disgusting.

In the midst of the 2017 NFL national anthem controversy, the sheriff of Bedford County, Mike Brown, erected a billboard near the county boundary on Route 460, proclaiming: "Law enforcement stands and places hand over heart for National Anthem! We kneel when we pray!" Residents interviewed by local WSET news remarked that it "showed law enforcement is behind the community." One resident said, "It shows respect for our country and the freedoms that we have, everything is related to that flag."

Old Glory, the symbol of freedom—and, now, our military—as it steadfastly waves "O'er the land of the free and the home of the brave." Who are the free and the brave whom Francis Scott Key is lauding? Key himself was a slaveowner, and the third stanza of his poem includes the lines "No refuge could save the hireling & slave / From the terror of flight or the gloom of the grave."

A. J. Willingham explains in a CNN online article that "in order to bolster their numbers, British forces offered slaves freedom in British territories in return for joining their cause. These black recruits formed the Colonial Marines and were looked down upon by people like Key, who saw their actions as treasonous."

Likewise, Colin Kaepernick and those who joined him were deemed treasonous for standing up against oppression. Protesting the national anthem was nothing new. As William Robin writes in the *New Yorker*, Kaepernick was joining a long history of protest. For example, in 1844, the abolitionist paper *The Liberator* published alternate lyrics for the national anthem that begin,

> Oh, say do you hear, at the dawn's early light
> The shrieks of those bondsmen, whose blood is now streaming.
> From the merciless lash, while our banner in sight
> With its stars, mocking freedom, is fitfully gleaming.

The rest of the lyrics, Robin continues, "describe slave ships waving 'our star-spangled banner,' excoriate 'our blood-guilty nation,' and conclude with the line 'O'er the death-bed of Freedom—the home of the slave.'"

Ironically, the military itself, since President Truman integrated it in 1948, has seen much more success in achieving racial equality than the larger society has. In 2008, *Newsweek* magazine reported that a comprehensive study by Jennifer Lundquist, a sociologist at the University of Massachusetts at Amherst, found that "the armed forces' social hierarchy—explicitly based on rank—overrides many of the racial or gender biases in civil society." According to Lundquist, "it's not that the military environment treats white males less fairly; it's simply that, compared to their peers in civilian society, white males lose many of the advantages that they had."

That might well be the case. Still, black Americans have a fraught history with both the American flag and state-sponsored violence. James Baldwin writes in *Notes of a Native Son* about the parents of black men in the army during World War II, how they "felt, mainly, a sense of peculiar kind of relief when they knew their boys were being shipped out of the south, to do battle overseas." He writes that it was "like feeling that the most dangerous part of a dangerous journey had been passed and that now, even if death should come, it would be with honor and without the complicity of their countrymen." To decry black Americans' protest as un-American, as somehow an attempt to denigrate American soldiers, is to deny their real historical experiences, to place a racial wall around who gets to enjoy full citizenship, even now.

When I was young, watching Westerns, I always sympathized with the Indians, and I did not know why. Maybe because our family mythology—true or not—included a full-blooded Cherokee Indian not too far back in the family tree. All my life I have rooted for the underdog, wanted the bullied to rise up, to prevail over their bullies. The source of my ambivalence as I sailed with my platoon to war was the dawning realization that I was not on the right side of that issue.

Sure, the US military has been a force for good in the world—defeating white supremacist Nazis, standing down Soviet communism—and I would not want to diminish the magnitude of that. This nationalism—let's be honest, ethno-nationalism—that holds up both our nation and our military as that "shining city on a hill" is an attempt to avoid a full and honest coming to terms with who we truly are as a people.

Serving in Desert Storm, I did not feel like a warrior for truth and justice. I did not feel the existential weight I longed for, that grounding sense of purpose like the one my father got from serving God. I felt like a faceless helmet in a vast and deadly wind, a nameless face in formation with thousands identical to me, sent out to maintain the primacy of the Empire. In her poem "The Summer Day," Mary Oliver asks, "Tell me, what is it you plan to do / With your one wild and precious life?" Sitting in the desert among all the death and destruction, my answer to that question was, "Not this."

For Christmas 2014, my sister bought us all tickets to a special Christmas concert. Well into the show, with the American flag on display, the singer called out for anyone who "has served, is serving now, or has a loved one serving" in the US military to stand. Almost half the mostly white, mostly Christian crowd stood. He serenaded them with a reverent rendition of "America the Beautiful." I did not stand. I stared at the flag and waited.

Capital T

THE SWAMPY WOODS MY MOTHER called "the bottom" and later "the clearing" spread to the north of Elkview Baptist Church. It lay beside the creek and the river, and every couple of years a heavy rain drove muddy brown water up into the trees, and the bottom looked like a real alligator swamp for a few days. Dad's church bought the property, cleared the trees, and with a bulldozer rerouted the winding creek to a straight path down at the far edge of the property. They graded it into a flat field, put up a softball backstop, and built a picnic shelter on the hill above it. After this, Mom started calling it "the clearing," even after everyone else had called it "the ballfield" for years.

When we were young, Vaughn and I trudged through sucking mud, playing in those swampy woods. We stomped through the creek, chasing ducks, and carefully turned over rocks, catching crawdads. Froze in fear when copperheads resolved from sticks and leaves at our feet. One day I was down there alone and found a duck's nest with two eggs. I stole one, carried it up from the bottom, and threw it at the church's kitchen door. The egg flew wide and exploded into the faded maroon of the painted bricks.

Only minutes later, Mom emerged from the church kitchen. She looked at the egg running down the church wall.

"Did you do this?" she asked.

"No." My heart sank. I was not a liar. I was a boy who told the truth.

"Who did it?"

"I don't know."

She stood with her hands on her hips and stared at me. She knew I had done it, and I knew she knew. I also knew she had not seen me, or we would have been having a very different exchange.

"You did not do it?" she asked.

"No." I knew the fear on my face betrayed my guilt.

"You are telling me the truth?"

I nodded.

She stared at the egg for an excruciating moment. It ran slowly down the faded maroon wall. I was the only other person anywhere near. She knew I was lying, and I knew she knew. She turned and gave me a withering stare. I stared wide-eyed back. It was too late to turn back and confess, so I waited it out.

Of all the kinds of lies I knew of at the time—white lies, black lies, lies of commission, lies of omission, exaggeration, deception—I had told the worst kind. I had told a barefaced lie, stood and looked right into my mother's eyes and insisted something was true when we both knew it was false.

By that age, I had heard countless preachers call upon "capital-T Truth." Since before I started the AWANA program, I had been memorizing Bible verses. I could already call them up topically by memory—a skill admired in young preacher boys. "Lying lips are an abomination to the Lord," Proverbs warns. "Ye shall know the truth and the truth shall set you free," Jesus says. He tells Pilate, "I have come into the world to testify to the truth," and Pilate asks him, "What is truth?" He does not answer Pilate, but he does tell his disciples, "I am the way, the truth, and the life." If we would follow Jesus, we can only do it in wisdom and in truth. Paul admonishes the Ephesians to "speak every man truth with his neighbor . . . let no corrupt communication proceed out of your mouth."

It was clear that by lying I was stepping from the side of good and right directly into the realm of the evil one. Jesus tells those who do not believe him they are on Satan's side, and that Satan "does not stand in the truth, because there is no truth in him. When he speaks a lie, he speaks from his own resources, for he is a liar and the father of it."

I knew I did not want to be on Satan's side because, as Paul states clearly to the Romans, "The wrath of God is being revealed from heaven against all the godlessness and wickedness of people, who suppress the truth by their wickedness."

Absolute was the word most associated with our truth. Absolute values. Moral absolutes. Preachers called it "capital-T Truth" as they made my tribe's case against the intellectual forces of the enemy. "Truth is like a lion," a member of my tribe posted on his Facebook page many years later, with the picture of a majestic male lion. "It does not need to be defended, only to be set free."

Pluralism was of the Enemy. Relativism was of the Enemy. All truth claims had to fit somehow into our premillennial dispensational worldview or they were from the Father of Lies, the Devil himself. Science was of the Devil because it sought to tear down our worldview, our tribal mythology.

In *Narrative, Religion and Science: Fundamentalism versus Irony, 1700–1999,* Stephen Prickett defines myths as "the stories we tell ourselves to make sense of the disparate and fragmented state of knowledge. It is not their truth but their task that is important." Prickett writes, "Our tribal stories . . . have in the past always given us a sense of who we are, where we ultimately belong. But whereas it was once our principal way of knowing . . . this is no longer true."

What happens if, in response to scientific and critical evidence that your tribal myths are not factual, you turn, as my tribe did, to science and criticism to prove they are indeed historically and scientifically accurate—maintaining that they happened in real time and space, just as written in the Bible? What does it do to your psyche if you must redouble your defense of those myths, even as science and higher criticism lay them bare as not facts but myths in Prickett's sense? Every new piece of scholarship becomes an attack to parry, every scholar an enemy to battle.

On March 6, 1991, President George H. W. Bush declared the advent of a "new world order." In the same speech, the president admonished that, surely, "if we can selflessly confront evil for the sake of good in a land so far away," we could take care of a few domestic problems. The ground war in Kuwait lasted only four days, after which we set up camp and waited to be loaded up and shipped home to the other side of the world, where those "few domestic problems" were the drumbeats of the culture war.

Ambivalent as I was about my part in the war, and in the military, and longing for some kind of purpose, I struggled to know what I would do with my life when I got home. I still felt a deep longing for connection to the Ultimate Other, the grand purpose, to live in service to something I believed worthy of my "one wild and precious life." My tribe's mythology was *myth* as Prickett defines it, and their angry insistence that it was historical fact made me cringe. It was not the hill I was going to die on.

Then I ran across a book, as I browsed through the bookstore in the Christian Servicemen's Center in Olongapo City, Philippines. That book was Francis Schaeffer's *A Christian Manifesto*. Schaeffer's photo on the back cover was not an author's head shot, but the full man sitting on a rock in front of a calm sea. He was a strange-looking man with a goatee, who still wore knickers, though, as far as I knew, grown men did not wear knickers even when they were the style. Still, I read the book in one sitting.

This was Schaeffer's response to *The Communist Manifesto* and *The Humanist Manifesto I* and *II*. Published in 1981, *A Christian Manifesto* called for conservative white evangelicals to rise up and practice civil disobedience in the face of godless government policies. Schaeffer allowed that we could ally with other groups that were "co-belligerents" against the overstepping government.

This civil disobedience "is biblical," Schaeffer writes, "because any government that commands what contradicts God's law abrogates its authority. It is no longer our proper legal government, and at that point we have the right and the duty to disobey it." His admonition: "There does come a time when force, even physical force, is appropriate." University of Virginia sociologist James Davison Hunter had recently popularized the term *culture wars* to describe this conflict, and Pat Buchanan raised it as his campaign flag. By the time I finished the book, I was convinced this was my calling.

Back home, I ordered Schaeffer's collected writings. The five books arrived in a shrink-wrapped set, and their bright, distinct colors— blue, green, yellow, orange, red—seemed to be an indication of the clear, categorical, Scottish common-sense realism inside. In *Escape from Reason*, Schaeffer writes about "true truth" which, grounded in God, is absolute and reliable.

The Soviet Union was crumbling, which was good, but back home truth was under assault from the twin evils of relativism and pluralism. As my tribe saw it, pluralism was not just a call to live together with people of many different belief systems, as is necessary in a *pluralistic* society. It was the argument that there were belief systems no less legitimate than our own. Relativism meant to my tribe that since there were so many different systems and no one universal paradigm anymore, people could simply choose what was right and wrong for themselves.

To relativism and pluralism, Francis Schaeffer said a firm *not so.* Truth existed no matter how postmodernists in the West hacked at it. In a tribute to Schaeffer, delivered in 2014 at Round Church, Oxford, Christian writer and lecturer Os Guinness quoted George Orwell: "When you get to a place where there is so much deception and lies, telling the truth is a revolutionary act." He concluded his tribute with a challenge: "As followers of Jesus," [conservative] Christians are called "to stand for truth and to be people of truth where telling the truth is becoming a revolutionary act."

The months after my return from Operation Desert Storm were a heady time for me. All my questions about our mythology did not go away, but I had a new purpose—and, as anyone who has struggled to get free of an oppressive belief system will understand, my path out was not a straight march. Almost everyone I knew and cared about was there, and for that reason I desperately wanted to believe things I found unbelievable.

After devouring Schaeffer's collection, I married Julie, and the two of us set off for Lynchburg, where Julie would finish her undergraduate degree at Liberty University and I would train in the seminary to be a fighter for capital-T Truth. We found an apartment that would take dogs. We bought a black-and-white English springer spaniel and named him Zeke. I took a job in a juvenile lockup, and Julie worked in the human resources department at LU. We labored away at school and work, and had a date night every Friday night. I set aside my studies, we ordered pizza, and watched a new TV show called *Cops*. We renamed the show "Bad Boys," after the intro song.

The human resources office was located on the first floor of a dormitory building. Julie tabulated time cards for payroll and fielded worker's compensation claims. One day Falwell came through to talk to the new director, a woman who was either his cousin or his niece—Julie was not sure which. He glanced at Julie on his way through, but did not speak. Julie's natural and unique beauty was striking even on a campus full of students who were, boys and girls alike, pretty. Several days later, the human resources director called a meeting with Julie and asked her to move up to the mansion and be Falwell's receptionist, sit right outside his heavy office door.

The mansion that housed Falwell's office and the senior staff was a modified Georgian Revival–style house. (US senator Carter Glass had built it in 1923 and named it Montview.) While Julie was in the mansion, the front doors stayed open. From behind the receptionist's desk in the wide front hall, she could see, through the glass storm door, the valley below—a mostly wooded stretch of Route 29 then, now a congested Ward's Road full of strip malls and franchise restaurants—and, on the hill across it, Central Virginia Community College. The desk was in the middle of everything, though, in the way of anyone coming or going. Out in the open, exposed. To the right were the wide steps to the upstairs administrative offices. To the left was the heavy black door with a special punch padlock above the knob. That was Falwell's office, the inner sanctum, the seat of power.

Julie was never supposed to bother Falwell with phone calls. His secretary decided which calls were important enough for him, and Julie was not to disturb her with any but the most urgent calls. Julie's short stint at the mansion was during a time when the school was going through a financial crisis and appeared to be hurtling toward bankruptcy. Then, as Robert Parry reported in a 1997 *Los Angeles Times* article, Falwell traveled to South Korea and begged self-proclaimed messiah and conservative donor Sun Myung Moon for a life-saving cash infusion.

Moon's claim to be a messiah was not enough of a problem to keep Falwell from accepting his help. He had the money Falwell needed, so an under-the-table alliance was forged. They funneled the money through a foundation called the Women's Federation for World Peace. Parry writes, "On Jan. 28, 1995, during his nationally televised 'Old Time Gospel Hour,' Falwell credited the directors of the foundation,

Daniel A. Reber and Jimmy Thomas, with saving Liberty. Falwell made no mention of his more prominent financial angel, Moon." The dining hall at Liberty is named after Reber and Thomas, not Sun Myung Moon. Moon's longtime associate Ron Godwin moved to Lynchburg and joined the senior administration at Liberty University.

According to Dirk Smillie's *Falwell Inc.: Inside a Religious, Educational, Political, and Business Empire*, Godwin became Falwell's closest advisor. Godwin met with him every morning at Bob Evans to have breakfast and strategize. A bully even in decrepitude, Falwell liked to menace his waiter with surprise fist jabs to the gut. At one of these meetings, Godwin pitched an idea: start an online school like the University of Phoenix. Falwell loved the idea, so Godwin ran with it. This turned out to be a cash cow, and according to Nick Anderson, writing for the *Washington Post*, by the end of 2012 it took Liberty University from financial insolvency to "[one] billion in net assets for the first time, counting cash, property, investments and other holdings."

While Julie sat answering phones and greeting visitors outside Falwell's door in the mansion, before Sun Myung Moon rode to the rescue, the senior administration was in a panicked frenzy upstairs. Outside financial advisors tromped in, and there was a small scandal because many of them were not Christians. Shortly on their heels came buildings and grounds workers with shredding machines. Everyone in the mansion sat with stacks of paper, garbage bags, and a shredder—including Julie at her receptionist desk. At one point, Falwell walked by her desk as she shredded and boomed down at her, "You are not reading those!"

She assured him that she was not, and she did not. She shredded documents without looking at them, filled garbage bags with shredded documents. She sat and fielded endless calls from panicked Christians who had sacrificed to buy bonds in support of the school. More than a few investors abused her over the phone in their anger.

Julie shredded documents along with senior staff, and I sat in class during the day learning Hebrew, Greek, church history, and homiletics, after which I worked shifts at the juvenile lockup. It was late when Julie met me with her horror stories of unsavory—and possibly even illegal—goings-on in the mansion. She grew more bitter by the day, and came to despise everyone at the mansion.

One day she accompanied the secretary to an old warehouse building on Carroll Avenue, beside Route 29, near where the school still holds its traditional Halloween haunted maze, Scaremare, every fall, and the two of them loaded up more boxes of records to be shredded. She discovered that there were also stacked boxes—box after box, containing hundreds of books, maybe more—full of copies of Falwell's autobiography. The secretary told her that the school had purchased them in order to push the book up the Christian bestseller chart.

"Is that ethical?" she asked me that night in our apartment.

"Doesn't seem like it," I said.

"Is it illegal?"

"I don't know."

"I don't know if all that shredding is, either," Julie said.

We did not discuss it further. We were both tired.

In less than a month, Julie requested a move back down to human resources, and the mansion staff agreed—pretty as she was, they agreed she was not a good fit.

Julie's experience up at the mansion continued to eat at her; it ate at me, too, though I did my best to defend Falwell to my disenchanted wife. Then, one day in class, one of my fellow students complained that when he counted attendance on Sunday mornings at Thomas Road Baptist Church, his supervisor told him Falwell wanted the attendance swollen with creative math.

"Isn't that lying?" he asked the seminary professor.

The professor went into a long response in which he said, "All great leaders lie." Falwell was accomplishing great things for the cause, and the mission was much larger than he was, anyway—this was an all-out war and when you march to war, you have God's blessing to change the rules of moral and ethical behavior, particularly, though not exclusively, in the use of lies.

Another of my seminary professors elucidated this for the class. He called it the doctrine of the ruse de guerre, the trick of war: it is moral to do whatever is necessary to win when you are at war and the war is just, and, conversely, failing to win by any means necessary amounts to a moral failing.

"Like Stormin' Norman," the professor told us, referring to General Norman Schwarzkopf's use of inflatable tanks to fool Saddam Hussein in Operation Desert Storm, which was still fresh in everyone's memory.

The professor went on to appeal to the doctrine of the ruse de guerre to justify all the horrific things ancient Israel did to its enemies as well. Those who disagreed with my tribe's version of moral absolutes were the avowed enemies of God, and we had to defeat them by any means necessary.

From there, it devolved to the intentional use of lies to bolster their preferred narrative. In a May 2017 *Vox* article titled "Donald Trump and the Rise of Tribal Epistemology," David Roberts relates the story of "Climategate," in which emails were hacked at a climate research facility, cut, edited, and stripped of context in order to make it look like the scientists were up to something nefarious. No fewer than five investigations cleared the scientists of wrongdoing. Nevertheless, "by then, for a large class of right-wing media consumers, it was already settled history, part of shared lore."

Donald Trump waved his avarice and greed, he disparaged the poor and weak, he bragged of his sexual predation. News and social media were rife with evidence of the man's narcissism and amorality. He was a brazen con man (Trump University, for just one example). He was also a pathological liar.

David Leonhardt and Stuart Thompson had a running list in the *New York Times* of what they simply called "Trump's Lies," starting when he took office on January 20, 2017. His supporters complained that the *Times* should do the same for Barack Obama because, as the refrain goes, "all politicians lie." The *Times* took them up on it and discovered that "in his first 10 months, Trump told nearly six times as many falsehoods as Obama did during his entire presidency."

Leonhardt and Thompson reminded readers, "Trump's political rise was built on a lie (about Barack Obama's birthplace). His lack of truthfulness has also become central to the Russia investigation, with James Comey, the former director of the FBI, testifying under oath about Trump's 'lies, plain and simple.'" Their conclusion: "There is simply no precedent for an American president to spend so much time telling untruths. Every president has shaded the truth or told occasional whoppers. No other president—of either party—has behaved as Trump is behaving. He is trying to create an atmosphere in which reality is irrelevant."

In *The Fellowship of the Ring*, part 1 of the film trilogy by Peter Jackson based on J. R. R. Tolkien's *The Lord of the Rings*, the wizard Saruman asks his colleague Gandalf to join him in serving the evil wizard Sauron. Their world is undergoing great change, he argues, power structures are shifting, old ways passing and new ways growing to take their place. He tells Gandalf they must rule this new age. "But we must have power," Saruman says, "power to order all things as we will." The only way to make sure good prevails, he assures Gandalf, is to obtain power. The only way to obtain power is to make an unholy alliance with the evil Sauron: "A new power is rising . . . We may join with that Power . . . There is hope that way. Its victory is at hand; and there will be rich reward for those that aided it. As the Power grows, its proved friends will also grow; and the Wise, such as you and I, may with patience come at last to direct its courses, to control it. We can bide our time, we can keep our thoughts in our hearts, deploring maybe evils done by the way, but approving the high and ultimate purpose: Knowledge, Rule, Order; all the things we have striven so far in vain to accomplish, hindered rather than helped by our weak and idle friends. There need not be, there would not be, any real change in our designs, only in our means." By this time, infected with Sauron's evil, Saruman is mad with his own desire for power.

My tribe opted not to speak truth into a changing culture; they chose political power, and in the 2016 election, they came out and waved their selling-out for the world to see. They repeated the refrain that Trump "tells it like it is," and I wondered how in the hell they could say such a thing. To them, his lies either were immaterial to their war and so of no concern, or tucked nicely into their tribal mythology and advanced their cause. Therefore, instead of standing up and insisting on being people of truth, they flocked to support a man of whom we can justly say, he is a liar and the truth is not in him. They made a deal with the devil. How can they ever again call themselves people of small-t truth, much less people of capital-T Truth?

My White Tribe

W HEN MY DAUGHTER GRACE WAS a rising sophomore in high
school, one of her summer reading assignments for first term
was Richard Wright's *Black Boy*. Both of her older siblings, Evan
and Asher, had read it for English class as well. In an autobiograph-
ical sketch, Wright speaks of the "dread of being caught alone upon
the streets in white neighborhoods after the sun has set." He says,
"While white strangers may be in these neighborhoods trying to get
home, they can pass unmolested. But the color of a Negro's skin . . .
makes him suspect, converts him into a defenseless target." Reading
Wright's book, my daughter got a glimpse into what it was like to be
a black boy in the United States some three-quarters of a century ago.

I never read *Black Boy* in school. I cannot remember being as-
signed a single black writer until I chose an African American literature elective my junior year in college. I was raised in a place that was
not only lily-white, but white with a red neck. No black people lived up
the Elk River until a white woman and her black husband moved with
their children into a trailer beside Route 119, between Elkview and
Clendenin. From passing cars, people hurled slurs and rocks at the
children as they tried to play in the yard or waited for the school bus.
Kids laughed about it in the halls of Herbert Hoover High School.
Eventually someone burned a cross in their front yard—at least, that
was the story I heard—and the family moved away. People of color did
not often venture up the Elk River, not willingly.

My world was even more circumscribed than redneck Elk River
culture. Inside Elkview Baptist Church, we gazed out with suspicion at every passing fad, television show, and popular song. Everywhere and at all times, Satan was trying to sneak his subversive message into our home. We had to be diligent. So, along with virtually

everything else unfamiliar, nonwhite evangelicals were different, and therefore suspect.

White evangelical Christians, by definition, could not allow nonwhite Christians to join the tribe. They did allow nonwhites to come around for worship and fellowship, within reason, as long as they behaved in an appropriately white-evangelical way. Acceptable nonwhite Christians—born again and in doctrinal, political, and social agreement with my tribe—fit into two basic groups: black believers, and nonwhite-other-race believers. The only times I ever saw nonwhite-other-race believers up the Elk River was as object lessons carted in by one missionary or another, a curiosity to marvel over. It was a 1970s version of the Victorian "white man's burden."

Because a black born-again family sent their children up the Elk River from Charleston to Elk Valley Christian School, I became good friends with several of them. I played football and soccer with them, chummed with them in the hallways and classrooms. What I could not fully understand back then was how difficult it was for Doug, Tammy, Donald, and Steve, riding every day on the green EVCS bus with kids that Tammy, in a conversation many years later, referred to as "country-ass creekers." Not a single day went by for them without taunts from open racists. In addition, there was the continuous stream of what would now be called microaggressions from those who meant well but knew no better.

On a long ride home from a football game in seventh grade, Donald and I sat together in the dark bus, outside lights flashing across our faces. The bus reeked of sweat and diesel, and the plastic bus seat in front of us was cracked and dry. I talked of a job I'd been doing since sixth grade, picking up garbage in the parking lot of the Goody Shop down the street in Elkview. They paid me seventy-five cents and a milkshake of my choosing. I usually got cherry because it finished with a pile of chopped-up maraschino cherries in the bottom, slippery and chewy and sweet enough to make your stomach hurt. Sometimes I brought my brother or a friend to help pick up all the trash, and the shop owners, the parents of a former classmate from my days in public school, would pay us in money and milkshakes. I remember them as kind and generous people.

Donald and I talked about other things. Because the bus ride from Ohio Valley Christian School was a long one, we eventually fell silent and listened to the cheerleaders harmonizing beautifully, but for far too long, on the *nana nananana* part of Journey's "Loving, Touching, Squeezing."

"If I lived in Elkview," Donald said after a long stretch, "we would do that Goody Shop job together, wouldn't we?"

"Yeah," I said. "We would."

At that point, I felt a rush of deep affection for my friend. I knew, even then, that life would be dangerous for Donald if he lived up in Elkview. I was not angry or outraged—I had no idea it could be any different—but I was deeply sad for my friend sitting on the bus there beside me.

I had the same affection for Steve, Doug, and Tammy that I had for Donald. They were in my core group of friends until I left Elk Valley Christian School, trying to get away from oppression of the religious kind. I loved them, but I remember hearing white students say things like, "Hey man, who hit you and blacked your face?" and "What's worse than a face full of zits? One blackhead." I cannot remember coming to their defense. It was the water we swam in, and I had no idea the world was different anywhere else.

In 1955, a white woman in Mississippi accused a black boy, Emmett Till, of whistling at her. White men dragged Till from his cousin's house in the middle of the night, strung him up in a barn, beat him, and gouged out one of his eyes. He was defiant, cursed the white men who tortured him, so they shot him dead, tied a 70-pound fan to his neck with barbed wire, and threw his carcass into the river. That's what it was like for a black boy in 1955.

After the death of Jerry Falwell Sr. in 2007, Max Blumenthal published an article titled "Agent of Intolerance" in *The Nation*, exposing the depth of Falwell's racism. In 1958, for example, Falwell preached a sermon "Segregation or Integration, Which?" In the sermon, he said,

"When God has drawn a line of distinction, we should not attempt to cross that line." He warned that integration "will destroy our race eventually." For shock value, he added, "In one northern city, a pastor friend of mine tells me that a couple of opposite race live next door to his church as man and wife."

Falwell Sr. was an outspoken opponent of racial integration, and vocally supported former Virginia governor and US senator Harry Flood Byrd's plan to employ "massive resistance" to school desegregation by closing down whole school districts. Falwell was the first chaplain of the group formed to resist integration in Lynchburg, and offered the closing prayer after one school superintendent gave a speech encouraging opposition to integration in the name of states' rights. J. Edgar Hoover produced anti–civil rights literature; Falwell helped distribute it. In a sermon titled "Ministers and Marchers," Falwell impugned the "sincerity and nonviolent intentions of some civil rights leaders, such as Dr. Martin Luther King Jr., Mr. James Farmer, and others, who are known to have left-wing associations." Falwell preached, "It is very obvious that the Communists, as they do in all parts of the world, are taking advantage of a tense situation in our land, and are exploiting every incident to bring about violence and bloodshed."

In 1963, when white supremacist Alabama governor George Wallace backed down from his stand against desegregation at the University of Alabama, he resumed the struggle under the banner of resistance to the federal government's infringement on states' rights. Falwell Sr. followed Wallace into the struggle for small government and states' rights. He continued to rail against the civil rights movement, now in terms not of racial integration but of outsider interference, saying that he would not be "bullied and attacked by white Northern demonstrators" who "demand we follow their dictates."

In 1985, Falwell traveled to South Africa and schmoozed with its white supremacist government leaders who were under increasing international pressure to end apartheid. Upon his return, he praised the white supremacists, and said of the Anglican bishop Desmond Tutu, a leader in the movement for racial justice in South Africa, "If Bishop Tutu maintains that he speaks for the black people of South Africa, he's a phony." He went on to urge conservative Christians to support the white government by buying South African gold coins and investing in companies that operated there. He also spoke out publicly against freeing the black anti-apartheid activist Nelson Mandela, a future president of South Africa, from prison.

In the early 1990s, when I attended seminary at Liberty University, there were more South Koreans in my classes than black Americans. For all the school's rebranding, the black community had still not forgotten its founder's civil rights record. One of the few black students was a man whose first name was Hiawatha. He educated me. He told me to watch how people reacted to him, and I did, hanging back so their reactions wouldn't be mitigated by the presence of a clean-shaven white guy in a shirt and tie. Indeed, people gave him nervous glances in convenience stores. The young white girls at school gave him a wide berth in the hallways. I was astonished. Hiawatha shrugged it off in weary resignation.

Hiawatha became president of the graduate student body after the faculty deemed the elected president unfit to serve because he had been divorced. A charismatic speaker, Hiawatha received invitations to preach all over the South, and the administration eventually offered him a staff position upon graduation.

We discussed it over lunch one day, and he said to me, "I don't want to be their token black."

"What are you talking about?" I said. "They love you."

"Yeah?" he said, looking hard into my eyes. "Let me try to date one of their daughters."

My first job after graduating from seminary was teaching in a small Christian school in West Union, Ohio. Julie and I moved there in the summer of 1995. We rented a small farmhouse with an attic full of mud dauber nests and a tobacco barn across the yard. Some of the local kids were out of school for two weeks at a time to harvest and hang tobacco. It was nice to go out and stand under the curing leaves, breathe in their thick, sweet aroma.

There was a significant homeschooling community in West Union. It had connections to the small school where I taught, and homeschooling mothers would pay me for tutoring their children in

English, one of them paying with fresh eggs, still stained and flecked with chicken manure.

I taught seventh- through eleventh-grade English. Once a girl in my seventh-grade class asked me if I would bump her test grade up a letter in return for an apple pie. "No," I told her, "but a blueberry pie . . . ?" The next day, she came back with another girl, brought me a blueberry pie she had baked herself, and told me she knew I would not change her grade and did not expect me to, but she just wanted to bake me a pie. She was a delightful young woman.

Her brother was in my eleventh-grade class and was the big man on campus. He was not a particularly gifted student, but he managed. He was earnest and upright, just like his father, who was a straight-talking farmer. This boy's dream was to go to the police academy and become an Ohio state trooper. He was also fascinated with Adolf Hitler—read about him, talked about him, wrote essays about him. He stopped me in the hallway one day to announce he had discovered Hitler's true name had been Schicklgruber. (His research was not quite accurate, as Schicklgruber was actually the name of Hitler's paternal grandmother.) "No wonder he changed his name," the young man—already a full 2 inches taller than I was, with his straight, brown hair cut neat and high—said as he laughed.

We attended a small Baptist church in West Union and formed a bond with a family who was homesteading in the hills outside town. We had them over for dinner, and the husband and I hit it off, talked as men do, interrupting one another in our excitement about home-steading. I told him what I'd read about it, which, beyond visiting the local Amish, was all I had done; he told me what he and his wife were actually doing. Our wives sat and listened. He took it further than I would have, talked of fences, weapons, and observation towers, so that when the global meltdown came, people fleeing the cities could not overrun them.

As Julie's belly grew large with our first child, Evan, we grew close to this couple. So close that when they learned they would have to go to Florida for an extended time—his father owned a trucking com-pany that specialized in oversized loads, and they had contracted work down there—they offered to let us stay at their homestead at no charge. They even offered to paint the rooms to suit us and to designate one for Evan's nursery.

We were seriously considering the offer. One Saturday the husband asked if I would come over and help him pour a concrete slab for an eventual garage. While I was there, his wife would take Julie out for lunch and "girl time."

I arrived to find his father—who presided as a patriarch and received due deference from his boys—two brothers, and a couple of other men there, already working. Since I was an English teacher and not a real workingman, he told me I could patty and grill the burgers for lunch. In casual conversation during the meal, one brother remarked that his daughter had "outed" him to their pastor at church. She had told the pastor that he, her father, believed black people don't go to heaven. It was not long before the patriarch turned the conversation toward me and made quite clear what the brother meant.

"So you graduated from seminary?" he asked me.

"I did."

"Why do they call it a Master of Divinity?" he said. Not waiting for me to answer, he said, "It's ridiculous for someone to claim to be a master of divinity."

His smirk made it clear he knew the difference between God and a field of study; he was toying with me, so I did not bother with a reply. My friend and his brothers eyed me expectantly.

"Let me ask you something," the patriarch said. They all looked at me. "Does a Jew go to heaven?"

"Well . . ." I said. I had graduated from a Baptist seminary and I attended a Baptist church, but I had recently read Louis Berkhof's *Systematic Theology* and been convinced of the truth of Reformed Christian theology. I began to enunciate my understanding of the doctrines of grace.

"Wrong," he boomed over me.

I stopped and waited.

"A horse lives and dies in time," he said, "and a Jew lives and dies in time." As the brother had implied earlier about black people, he was telling me that he believed Jewish people had no souls. He was calling them animals.

I do not remember how I responded.

After eating, the men pulled out various automatic rifles and shot up milk jugs hanging at the edge of the yard, where it gave way to forest. I drove back to the farmhouse where Julie told me her day had been lovely. I told her about my day. Then we talked about the other people around town, some of them in the same Southern Baptist church we attended, who were friends with this couple, and who were also homesteading. The boy in my eleventh-grade class who wanted to be a cop and loved Hitler.

"We can't raise children in this place," Julie said.

I agreed.

After church the following Sunday, we met our new friend and his wife at Long John Silver's for lunch. I asked the man about his father's and brother's comments.

"We believe God chooses who will be his blessed people."

"I understand that," I said. "But it sounded to me like you believe it is racial."

He paused for a few long seconds. "We do," he said, looking straight into my eyes. "We do believe it is racial."

What followed was a frank exchange. He was vague when I asked him about religious affiliation, but he did tell me they believed they were part of the lost tribe of Israel and that ethnic Jews were impostors—or worse. The discussion ended with the understanding that the friendship we two couples had been cultivating was over. His wife cried. Julie grew so nervous she could not keep herself from laughing.

Back at the little farmhouse I so loved, Julie and I agreed it was time to leave. I did not sign the contract to stay on at the school. Evan was born on July 14, in Maysville, Kentucky. Two weeks later, we packed up and got the hell out of West Union, Ohio. I did not tell the pastor of the church we attended about the white supremacists in his congregation. I knew I should have but I did not.

We eventually settled back in Lynchburg, where we both still live. Moving back, we were confident that, though racism was obviously present, because black and white Americans lived more closely together in the South, there was not the treacherous white supremacy that lurked under the surface in the schools and churches of Adams County, Ohio.

Then Barack Obama won the White House, and my white tribe showed their true selves, tacitly condoning the racial resentment of the Tea Party, if not actively joining in. Some even bought into the racist conspiracy that the first black president was not a true citizen at all, but an impostor born in Kenya. Not only that, he was a secret Muslim with radical ties, bent on bringing down Christian America and imposing Sharia law.

Nevertheless, white as I was, I could afford to retain the naïveté that led me to believe racism was in decline. For years, I remained under the illusion that West Union was one of a shrinking number of outliers, isolated eddies of racist attitudes that the rest of the country had left behind. I grew away from the beliefs of my Baptist upbringing, and naturally found myself among liberal friends, though still most of them were white. We believed history was arcing toward justice.

When my children were still in high school, I was a taxi-dad for them and their friends. After I'd watched a documentary about food deserts titled *A Place at the Table*, I discovered that one youngster I saw relatively often was not only poor, but also lived with what we now euphemistically call "food insecurity." Not incidentally, this child was black.

All three of my children are musicians, and the circles in which they moved were as diverse as any you could find in Lynchburg. I found it heartening to see what appeared to be Martin Luther King Jr.'s dream of "little black boys and black girls . . . able to join hands with little white boys and white girls as sisters and brothers."

Outside school, things could get awkward fast. The disparity was undeniable—even if it was uncomfortable to acknowledge. One side of town was booming economically due in large part to the torrent of federal financial aid money pouring into nonprofit Liberty University. At the same time, Lynchburg's poverty rate was abysmal—for whites it was 19 percent, which is over 4 percent higher than the national average. The poverty rate for black citizens of Lynchburg was 30 percent. According to the city council's analysis in 2015, this poverty was intergenerational.

Just as it was with my friend Donald and me, my kids and their black friends were on paths that would likely split along racial lines as they grew into adulthood. My children do not have limitless opportunities—we live on teachers' salaries—but their family and social situations have placed them on a springboard that, if they choose to use it, will launch them into comfortable, middle-class lives. They will have to work hard, but their work will pay off, and they will have a financial safety net if they fail once or twice. Not so for many of their friends on the other side of the racial divide. Where my kids find a springboard, these friends too often find a fence and, behind it, a wall.

I get pushback from members of my tribe on this. They discuss this issue carefully because they do not want to be labeled as racist. Why do I hesitate even now to use the word, when racism—individual, institutional, and systemic—is such a massive and undeniable problem?

But is racism really an undeniable problem? When I ask this question, I inevitably get some variation on two defensive responses: "You are the one who is racist, because you think black people need handouts, can't be successful on their own merit" and "It is not fair to take away what I have earned fair and square and give it to someone else who refuses to work." In an online argument, one of my tribe—a member of my own family—ranted, "Excuses, blaming whites and one party voting will never allow the African American community to excel. Ditch Al Sharpton and Jesse Jackson and make some changes."

The root assumption of both these claims is that almost everyone starts with a similar array of opportunities, and some have squandered theirs, or at least not worked quite hard enough. This is simply not the case. In his *Atlantic* article "The Case for Reparations," Ta-Nehisi Coates gets to the point. He writes that "America was built on the preferential treatment of white people—395 years of it." It is not ancient history, either. We live in an America, he points out, "in which black college graduates still suffer higher unemployment rates than white college graduates, and black job applicants without criminal records enjoy roughly the same chance of getting hired as white applicants with criminal records."

I do not want my children's black friends—bright, beautiful, and talented kids—to curb their dreams to fit white America's definition of them. I do not want my own children to grow into the kind of white people who will someday run into these childhood friends in line at the movie theater and assume that the reason they themselves are better off—it is close to a statistical certainty they will be—is because they are smarter and have worked harder. I do not want my children and their black friends pulling apart into separate social circles, but I imagine it will happen.

I was at my first Pi party, thrown for the daughter of nerdy friends; she was turning three years, one month, and fourteen days old: 3.14. The house was decorated and festive, with hats for the guests on the entryway table that looked like Green Bay Cheesehead hats, except they were slices of pie—and tiaras for those who wanted to be princesses. The house was full of stereotypical academics—highly educated, opinionated, *liberal*—and their children. Though it was not on anyone's mind, I noted that the ethnicities represented were white, Latino, and Jewish, but none of the guests was black. Kids ran playing through the house, parents stood around having drinks and grazing at the dining room table, spread full as it was with pies both savory and sweet.

Then the new neighbor from across the street walked in, wearing a shirt that said on the back: "Better a wolf of Odin than a Lamb of God."

Here's what I knew about the neighbor at this point: He had a son who played well with our friends' daughter, and who was apparently a sweet and lovely child. I'd had a conversation with the man before, and found him to be perfectly pleasant, though the Donald Trump sign in his front yard and the Confederate flag spread across his garage door windows told me we would not be friends. He was from West Virginia, had spent time in Germany as an army brat, and returned there to live as an adult for a while.

Several months later, a new basketball hoop went up at the end of his driveway with a backboard that was a flag—the black-, white-, and red-striped flag that Germany used from 1866 to the end of World War I. The Nazi party used this flag, too, from 1933 until 1935, when Hitler made the swastika flag its one official flag.

I knew very little about Wolves of Odin. A local acquaintance of mine, a man who is a Western Orthodox priest but was once a hardcore fundamentalist, has two sons who are known around town for having left Christianity and started a cult called the Wolves of Vinland, which practices ancient European paganism as they understand it and calls for, among other things, animal sacrifice. They move among the twenty- and thirty-somethings here in town, and people generally look at them with bemused curiosity. They call themselves a "tribe of folkish heathen." Part of their rituals, and what seems a necessity of membership, is a fight club. Jack Donovan, a proponent of "masculinity and tribalism," writes admiringly about them in a blog post: "The Wolves of Vinland are becoming barbarians. They're leaving behind attachments to the state, to enforced egalitarianism, to desperate commercialism, to this grotesque modern world of synthetic beauty and dead gods. They're building an autonomous zone, a community defined by face-to-face and fist-to-face connections where manliness and honor matter again."

If the tribe were only a bunch of Luddites playing fight club in the woods, we could think about it in terms of the crisis of masculinity, or the effects of technology, but there is something deeper, and more sinister, going on.

Writing about the Wolves of Vinland for the *Daily Beast* in 2015, Betsy Woodruff reports that she asked them some questions on their Facebook page and "the group didn't dispute being characterized as white nationalist." She also reports that in pictures of the tribe she saw "T-shirts that read 'Free Hjalti,' a reference to Wolves of Vinland member Maurice Michaely who was sentenced to spend two and a half years in prison after pleading guilty to burning a historic black church." In a podcast by the Pressure Project, Paul Waggener, one of the Wolves' two founding brothers, said, "All this talk of equal living, equal rights, coexistence—fuck that shit." They have made the Southern Poverty Law Center's list of hate groups (one of almost nine hundred active hate groups in the United States as listed on the SPLC website).

At the Pi party that day, no one asked this man about his Wolf of Odin shirt. It is possible most of them did not know enough about white supremacy to recognize the shirt's meaning. Maybe they did not notice it at all, busy as they were rescuing free-playing toddlers from accidental harm. Maybe he found his way to these local Wolves of Vinland boys. Maybe he was striking out on his own religious path. At one point, explaining why he liked lager beer, he said, "I'm German," in a strong West Virginia accent.

Across town at Liberty University, some professors themselves were promulgating neo-Confederate arguments at least as recently as 2013. In a short video documentary posted on Vimeo that year, called "The Enduring Legacy of the Civil War," Liberty history professors linked the fight against same-sex marriage to the southern fight against the abolition of slavery—both characterized as the good Christian fight for states' rights against the evil encroachments of an overreaching federal government. Dr. Carey Roberts, for instance, in discussing the cause of the Civil War, had this to say: "What we saw happening from the 1820s to the 1830s and '40s is that one particular section of Americans, largely in New England, through various religious movements and activities really, really pitched a war against tolerance. And as a result of that—the breakdown of toleration, tolerating those things you dislike—Americans eventually start killing each other."

The result of all that killing in the Civil War? According to Professor Chris Jones, the Civil War was the beginning of the federal government's usurping of the states' rightful powers, and as a result, "we have all of us, us U.S. citizens that live in the United States, have increasingly become slaves so to speak."

Then Donald Trump, a promulgator of the racist lie that Obama was not a true American, ran for president. The overwhelming support of white evangelicals played no small part in securing his victory. Former grand wizard of the Ku Klux Klan David Duke declared on Twitter, "Make no mistake about it, our people have played a *huge* role in electing Trump!" Across town from me, Trump acolyte Jerry Falwell Jr. said, without apparent irony, "In my opinion, Donald Trump lives a life of loving and helping others as Jesus taught in the great commandment." This is around the same time that Falwell Jr. bragged about how he would take his gun and "end those Muslims."

In August 2016, a blistering report from the US Justice Department outlined a culture of racial bias in the Baltimore police department after all the officers involved in the death of a young black man named Freddie Gray were acquitted of any charges. This followed similar reports coming out of Seattle, Chicago, and Ferguson, Missouri. Members of my white tribe posted videos of police officers stopping black people and giving them ice cream, offered as evidence that black people were overreacting, being too sensitive.

On the news, after the death of another black man, Alton Sterling, at the hands of the police in Baton Rouge, his young son wept uncontrollably. He cried out, "Daddy!" That was the summer of 2016.

In 2017 white nationalism roared into the public square as symbols of the real—white—America. Pagan wolves, neo-Nazis, neo-Confederates, white nationalists wearing their new Trump-inspired uniform of white polo shirt and khaki pants, all marched together, their various flags subsumed by their shared guidon of whiteness. They chanted "Jews will not replace us" and "The South will rise again." They carried guns. They intended to intimidate, but, as became clear, they were itching for violence. What did they want, these white nationalists? To take the United States back to that culture in which Richard Wright tells us he could not walk in a white neighborhood without fear.

Sometimes I wonder about the white supremacist couple Julie and I knew back in West Union. Did they stay in Florida, or did they return to the hills outside West Union, armed and ready for battle? Are their children, grown now, carrying the white supremacist torch in places like Charlottesville? I wonder as well about the Hitler-obsessed boy who wanted to be a cop. Did he grow into a neo-Nazi? Is he patrolling the roads of Ohio? Have they all joined the other Trump-empowered white supremacists who have come out of hiding to declare their allegiances, or are they still keeping a low profile in the churches, schools, and police forces of our nation?

What is clear is that they are not outliers but are everywhere among us. I am not sure how to combat this, but I can no longer move away and pretend it is not my problem. At the very least, I must call it out where I see it. Donald Trump and those around him are white supremacists. The 80 percent of white evangelicals who support him find this acceptable. I believe it is worse than that; I believe that, notwithstanding their libertarian rhetoric of fairness and their Jesus-loves-everyone disclaimers, deep down where they might not even admit it to themselves, the tribe I grew up in is white supremacist to its core.

Man Up

I N THE MID-1970S, BEFORE THE textbook crisis hit Kanawha County and preachers all over the valley opened Christian schools in their church basements, I walked down the street every morning to Elkview Elementary School, which consisted of a new building and an old building linked by a breezeway, on the banks of the muddy Elk River. This was where I first encountered a girly man. The new principal at Elkview Elementary, Mr. Eagle, was somehow too neat, his mustache too crisp, his feathered bangs too perfect. His gait and gestures were not manly enough.

In my fifth-grade year, the textbook controversy boiled over, and my sister, brother, and I landed in Elk Valley Christian School. I have no idea how long Mr. Eagle stayed at Elkview Elementary. I do not know if he was gay, either; only that people whispered that he was—and if he was, something about him was so irreparably broken and disgusting that it could not be spoken of in polite company. As far as I could tell at the time, what was unacceptable about him was that he walked and talked a little too much like a woman.

"Alongside breadwinning and soldiering," Robert Self writes in *All in the Family*, "heterosexuality was another taken-for-granted dimension of American manhood." Anything else was unacceptable, even dangerous. Self writes, "The stereotypes of gay sexuality . . . veered between casting gay men as hyperfeminine and hypermasculine." They were either "weak, womanish and laughably unmanly," or they had "too much of the wrong kind of manliness," were "sexually voracious," "sexual predators" who "threatened children."

R. Marie Griffith shares in *Moral Combat: How Sex Divided American Christians and Fractured American Politics* the words of evangelical minister Tim LaHaye from his book *The Unhappy Gays: What Everyone*

Should Know about Homosexuality: "homosexuals were 'self indulgent, self-centered, undisciplined' people . . . they caused heartache to the good people around them, deceived others, despised women, lived only for sex, and skillfully recruited others into the fold." According to LaHaye, Griffith continues, "homosexuality was such a 'blight on humanity' and homosexuals themselves such immoral people that . . . many parents 'would prefer the death of their child to his adopting the unhappy wretchedness of homosexuality.'"

In the view of my tribe, these disgusting perverts were coming out of their closets, where they should have stayed, mounting an army to shout my frightened tribe into a closet of our own—they would not stop until we were hiding from persecution like early Christians in the catacombs. Jerry Falwell was onto them and sounded the alarm as he asked for money. In his book *Falwell Inc.*, Dirk Smillie shares a 1981 fundraising letter from Falwell Sr.:

> Dear Friend: I refuse to stop speaking out against the sin of homosexuality . . . I believe that the mass of homosexual revolution is always a symptom of a nation coming under the judgment of God. Recently 250,000 homosexuals marched in the streets of San Francisco. The homosexuals are on the march in this country. Please remember, homosexuals do not reproduce, they recruit, and many of them are after my children and your children. This is one major reason why we must keep *The Old Time Gospel Hour* alive . . . So don't delay. Let me hear from you immediately. P.S. Let me repeat, a massive homosexual revolution can bring the judgment of God upon this nation. Our children must not be recruited into a profane lifestyle.

My tribe cheered the orange-juice woman down in Florida, Anita Bryant, who was doing battle with an evil horde of homosexual perverts. Griffith recounts that Bryant "was tireless in describing 'militant homosexuals' as sick deviants bent on recruiting children and teens into their immoral and disgusting lifestyle." Griffith notes that Tim LaHaye (this time helped by his wife, Beverly) claimed in the book *The Act of Marriage* that "every homosexual is . . . capable of perverting many young people into his sinful way of life," and blamed "atheistic humanists and liberal institutions such as higher education and the entertainment industry." Atheists and liberals were responsible for "overturning centuries of opposition to homosexuality," which was allowing gays "to multiply tragically." Jerry Falwell Sr. said at a rally opposing gay rights, Griffith relates, "so-called gay folks would just as soon kill you as look at you."

It was up to my tribe, and our "cobelligerents," as Francis Schaeffer outlined, to save the world from gays and feminists. Though not yet named, the culture wars had begun. Gay men and lesbians were organizing, growing militant, preparing to mount an offensive against Christians. It was at Falwell's 1980 rally in Charleston, which I referred to in an earlier chapter, that we were supposed to encounter those militant lesbians.

Although I was a strong and athletic boy, I was small for my age. In addition, during my time at Elk Valley Christian School, I had run with boys who wore the latest clothes from Chess King in the new Charleston Town Center Mall and Ellis's over on the corner of Summers Street. Accordingly, I wore shiny dress pants, regular shirts with tux-shirt collars and skinny ties, shoes called Turtles that didn't tie but had Velcro straps, and striped suitcoats with the sleeves rolled up, which I bought at those same stores. This fashion sense did not travel upriver to Elkview. It didn't take long for me to learn that some of the boys there thought I had not just become something of a dandy, but had started wearing what they called "fag clothes."

When I left EVCS for Herbert Hoover High School, since I was the new kid, some of the girls befriended me, which made the boys jealous; since I was dressing in my clothes from Chess King and Ellis's, those dull, angry boys tormented me with slurs of "fag" and "faggot." As usual, I fought when I felt I could manage it, and I ran when I was outsized and outnumbered. I left EVCS for Herbert Hoover my sophomore year and returned to EVCS for the fall semester of junior year in order to play on their soccer team. Upon my return to Hoover in January of my junior year, the bullying began. For about six months during my senior year, the torment was relentless. I sawed off a chunk of heavy old mop handle, wrapped it in black electrical tape, and hid it in the weeds behind a telephone pole near Elkview Junior High. I carried an old bicycle handlebar stem, also wrapped in black tape, in my coat pocket. I never mustered the nerve to brandish either one. Even in high school, life for boys along the Elk River was still a *Lord of the Flies* world.

You would think that, having experienced bullying as I had, I would have empathized with the plight of gay men, but that would be giving me too much credit. In high school, my friends and I made sport of driving around Charleston shooting small darts into crowds. We had an air pistol that shot little silver darts with blue, red, and yellow plastic feathers. We didn't target any group for shooting—sometimes we shot BBs at each other from air rifles—but among the crowded places where we shot people was a gay bar called the Grand Palace.

We rode around Charleston drinking beer, swinging over through Kanawha City to cruise the strip and meet girls. We drove by the Cinema 7 between movies and shot darts at people. We hung out in the Kanawha Mall parking lot drinking beer. We drove by the Grand Palace and shot darts at people. Someone must have called the police. We were not careful, but we were never caught. I don't know if the police looked for us.

When we bragged about the drive-by shootings to a youth leader at church, we only told him about riding by the gay bar. This man was not a paid youth pastor, only a church member who volunteered with the high school class. He gave us the obligatory lecture—what we were doing was wrong and dangerous, and we should stop—but the smirk playing at the edges of his mouth betrayed that he saw the fun in watching degenerates scramble and yell as you shot them with darts. We understood perfectly what that almost-smirk meant: some people were fair game, and they deserved what they got.

Cartoon books circulated among Baptist churches when I was young; many churches had tract displays to distribute them for free. No *Spider Man*, or *Archie*, or *Richie Rich*; our comics had titles like *Are Roman Catholics Christians?* or *Going Down?* or *A Demon's Nightmare*. The one that frightened me most when I was a kid was *This Was Your Life!* A man dies after living for himself instead of for God, and before an angel throws him into the lake of fire, he has to stand naked while the whole world watches a huge movie of all the shameful things he's ever done "No!" he shouts as his secret lust plays on screen for all to see. "Not that!"

In 1984, the year I graduated from high school, a comic called *The Gay Blade* hit church tract stands. It described "Satan's shadowy world of homosexuality," which it characterized as a seedy underground of "filth and brutality." The comic depicted "the homosexuals" as demon-possessed and dangerous predators whom God commanded the Israelites to "smite . . . utterly destroy," and show no "mercy unto them." It was the story of Lot in Sodom, of course. A panel near the end of the comic read, "New laws are encouraging Sodomites . . ." Under that was a drawing of a gay man grabbing another man, saying, "You're offended by gays. Are you some kind of bigot?" The helpless straight man struggled to free himself from the gay man's grasp, pleading, "Let go!"

One weekend in 1993, while Julie and I were both at Liberty University, we attended Thomas Road Baptist Church. LU campus cops were in the parking lot warning churchgoers that a gang of homosexual activists was going to picket the church, clog up the sidewalks and parking lot, and bully the congregation. Unlike the no-show "brute" lesbians at the state capitol when I was a kid, these activists showed up: a scraggly bunch of young women and a smattering of young men who might or might not have been gay. Maybe thirty people in all.

I could just imagine these girls on the previous Friday, sitting at circled desks in some dark high school classroom. It would have been club period, and they would have all talked at once, excitedly planning this very protest. Now, they carried signs and called out to churchgoers after the morning service. The campus cops stood in their dark blue uniforms, black pistols on their hips, keeping guard over Falwell's flock as they made their way to the parking lot. They watched the protesters with blank, expressionless stares from behind sunglasses. The day was bright and cold.

"Jesus taught love," a girl said to me as Julie and I made our way along the sidewalk. The girl was frail, a Vietnam-era army coat hung on her thin frame. I remember her hair being stringy and straight. She could have been a hippie from twenty years earlier. "Jesus did not teach hate," she said.

We did not respond, but walked on.

"If being gay was such a problem to Jesus, why did he forget to mention it?" she called out.

In *Jerry Falwell: An Unauthorized Profile*, published in 1981, William R. Goodman Jr. and James J. H. Price quote Falwell saying in a sermon, "In my age, we laughed at queers, fairies and anyone who was thought to be homosexual. It was a hideous thing and no one talked about it, much less ever confessed to being a homosexual." Falwell went on to gripe, "Now they're coming out of the closet."

Self writes that the "bedrock notion" of American manhood—breadwinning, soldiering, heterosexuality—was "thrown into contentious dispute in the second half of the 1960s." Gay men came out of the closet and "questioned both heterosexuality and conventional manhood, upending the most indomitable taboo of modern American life." Things were changing in the culture at large, but within my tribe—given that our views of manhood, womanhood, and family were based on inerrant scripture—we had to dig in. If our mythology was to remain complete, we could give no ground on any front, particularly this one.

When I had sailed with the Marines to the war with Iraq, I'd had the sinking feeling that I was not standing up against oppression but simply adding one pair of boots on the ground for an imperial force. There in that parking lot, a similar sinking sensation dropped into my gut: I was not standing up to bullies on behalf of persecuted Christians; there was no army of brute lesbians out to push good Christians around. I was on the side of the bullies. I lowered my head and walked on to the car.

In 2014, I saw on social media that the Southern Baptists had held a conference called "The Gospel, Homosexuality, and the Future of Marriage," during which the Baptists met for dialogue with members of the LGBTQ community. I read about the conference to see if anything had really changed.

It had, and it had not.

The most striking change was that the Southern Baptists were backing off their insistence that sexuality is a lifestyle choice. Albert Mohler, president of Southern Baptist Theological Seminary, in a grudging nod to science, admitted publicly at the conference that he was "wrong years ago when [I] said same-sex attraction could be changed." This admission has huge implications for practices such as the cruel and damaging gay reparative therapy.

Because of this shift, Southern Baptists were sounding the call to deal more charitably with the LGBTQ community. This was a significant change. Glenn Stanton, the director of family formation studies at Focus on the Family, a conservative Christian policy institute, had even written a book titled *Loving My (LGBT) Neighbor: Being Friends in Grace and Truth*. However, they still viewed homosexuality as, in Stanton's words, "a particularly evil lie of Satan." While the more honest Baptists have finally conceded that homosexuality is not something one just chooses willy-nilly, they still insist that, natural as the inclination is, it is a result of the Fall, a manifestation of the human tendency to sinfulness. Failing to resist same-sex attraction places one in a state of perverse rebellion against the creator of the universe.

This gives LGBTQ people within conservative white evangelical churches a keen awareness that they are considered ontologically lacking in ways that others are not—the line "Hey, we're all sinners here" notwithstanding. LGBTQ people who remain in their conservative churches have to admit that an essential aspect of their existence in the world renders them vile and disgusting to the almighty creator of the universe—and there is not one goddamn thing they can do to change it.

Because my conservative white evangelical tribe still believes that feminists and the LGBTQ community are causing the breakdown of the family, which will lead to the wrath of God and the ultimate destruction of our nation, it is incumbent on them to insist that their interpretation of scripture is the one everyone must follow. In an address to Liberty University Law School students in 2015, interim dean Rena Lindevaldsen made clear that this is what they believe: "Civil government only has the authority that God has established, so civil government, if it's acting rightfully within its authority, just like individuals, should be acting consistent with Scripture."

Some men in my tribe feel particularly threatened by what they see as a perversion of manhood—too womanly or too manly in the wrong way—and they do not oppose meeting it in an appropriately manly way: with violence. Self writes, "Tolerance of violence has long been a tenet of manhood. To retreat or wince in the face of violence is to reveal feminine weakness and unmanly cowardice."

Mat Staver, a former dean of Liberty University's Law School and founder of the Liberty Council, attacks the LGBTQ community with an astounding blend of zeal and ignorance. When discussing why same-sex marriage should be illegal in an appearance with Jim Schneider on the radio show "*Crosstalk*," he said, "We know male-male sexual relationships are notoriously harmful, physically as well as mentally, and also female-female, same kinds of things . . . It's harmful to the individuals and those harms ultimately affect those around because they're communicable and other kinds of serious and deadly diseases." Staver also represented Kentucky court clerk Kim Davis, who claimed that she was exercising her religious freedom when she refused to issue marriage licenses to same-sex couples.

During his tenure at Liberty University Law School, Staver trained Falwell's "pit bulls," young lawyers ready to take the culture wars into the courtrooms and government buildings. He also defended the missionary Scott Lively, whose ten-year campaign in Uganda was not to feed the hungry and clothe the poor, or even to convert people to Christianity, but to fight "genocidal" and "pedophilic" gays. Lively likens gay rights activities to "the Nazis and Rwandan murderers," and complains in an article on his website titled "The Death of Human Rights" that the movement is trying to crush Christians' religious liberty "under the heels of its pink jackboots." Lively does not just cross the line of Godwin's law of Nazi analogies with his pink jackboots reference, he blitzkriegs it, writing a book, *The Pink Swastika*, in which he argues that the Nazi high command was a gang of militant homosexuals, all the way up to the Führer himself. In an open letter to Vladimir Putin, Lively offers his "heartfelt gratitude that your nation has take [sic] a firm and unequivocal stand against this scourge by banning homosexualist propaganda in Russia."

Staver wholeheartedly agrees. In a radio broadcast, "Faith and Free-dom," he praised antihomosexuality laws in Russia, Uganda, and Ni-geria, and at a "Celebrate America" rally, he proclaimed that the grow-ing tolerance for members of the LGBTQ community was "moving into a direct attack on who God is." Staver maintained that marriage equality will be the "end of Western Civilization."

When the Center for Constitutional Rights brought a federal law-suit against Lively, charging him with crimes against humanity for fomenting and encouraging deadly anti-LGBT rhetoric and legislation in Uganda, Staver, and his Liberty Counsel, served as his defense. Judge Michael Posner dismissed the case in 2017, but not because it had no merit. In his ruling, Posner wrote, "Defendant Scott Lively is an American citizen who has aided and abetted a vicious and fright-ening campaign of repression against LGBTI persons in Uganda." Posner made clear that "anyone reading this memorandum should make no mistake. The question before the court is not whether De-fendant's actions in aiding and abetting efforts to demonize, intimi-date, and injure LGBTI people in Uganda constitute violations of in-ternational law. They do." The reason, Posner wrote, that he had no choice but to dismiss the case was because Lively's criminal actions took place outside the jurisdiction of his court. Staver celebrated it as a victory over a case intended to "intimidate an innocent pastor into silence." In the course of Staver's defense of Lively, Staver himself shrugged off the 2011 bludgeoning murder of Ugandan gay rights ac-tivist David Kato by claiming, "Kato tried to force [the man who killed him] to have sex." Staver's American-manhood lens transformed a sexual proposition—if indeed anything occurred at all, which is not a given—into attempted rape, one that apparently ended as it should have, just another sodomite with his skull bashed in.

Of his opinion on using violence in their battle against LGBTQ rights, even on the scale of warfare, Staver said on Moody Radio that the legalization of same-sex marriage "is the thing that revolutions literally are made of." He said allowing same-sex couples to marry "would be more devastating to our freedom, to our religious free-dom . . . than anything that the revolutionaries during the American Revolution even dreamed of facing."

These sentiments are not the ravings of a few nuts on the fringes of the far right. Erick Erickson, whom Molly Ball, writing for *Atlantic Monthly* in 2015, called the most powerful conservative in America, repeatedly refers to LGBTQ activists as terrorists. This quotation comes from his RedState.com blog: "Gay rights activists . . . have not turned physically violent. But they are intent on destroying any who disagree with them. They will take the homes, businesses, and life savings of any who defy them. They will use the tools of the state and mob action through boycotts, fear, and intimidation to make it happen. They will not kill but they will threaten and scare . . . The divide between Islamic extremists and gay rights extremists is at death. They meet on the line at destruction."

In November 2015, presidential candidates Ted Cruz, Mike Huckabee, and Bobby Jindal attended the National Religious Liberties Conference, an event hosted by a preacher who repeatedly reminded his followers that God's punishment for homosexuality is death. At that very conference, the preacher proclaimed, "Yes, Leviticus 20:13 calls for the death penalty for homosexuals." He continued, "Yes, Romans chapter one, verse thirty-two, the Apostle Paul does say that homosexuals are worthy of death." He then cried out, with his Bible in the air, "His words not mine!" and as his audience at the political rally broke into applause, he called out, "And I am not ashamed of the gospel of Jesus Christ."

When asked about the preacher's words, Ted Cruz, then considered the most serious presidential contender at the conference—who had himself complained about the "gay jihad" against Christians—could only muster in response that the call to murder LGBTQ humans was "not explicit." In a previous interview with activist Peter Labarbera, Cruz charged that President Obama was more concerned with "rare mass shootings that take place in this country from time to time than he is with the fact that the majority of Americans are under constant threat from gay rights terrorism."

After the terrorist attacks of September 11, 2001, Jerry Falwell Sr. went on Pat Robertson's television show and blamed the attacks not just on secularists, abortionists, and the ACLU, but on "the gays and the lesbians who are actively trying to make that an alternative lifestyle." Ignoring the historical realities of US involvement in the

Middle East, Falwell proclaimed to all those rising up to reject his moral categories, "I point the finger in their face and say 'you helped this happen.'" When called out in the press, he said that wasn't what he meant at all. Of course, it was what he meant. Mat Staver meant it, too. Bryan Fischer, Scott Lively, Peter Labarbera, James Dobson, Kevin Swanson, and Ted Cruz all meant it. The fact that attitudes toward LGBTQ rights have shifted dramatically in the United States does not mean these men will listen to reason, or consider evidence that calls their reading of scripture into question. They will not.

They feel they must remain diligent against an existential threat, keep this evil from infecting them. In January 2016, Franklin Graham, in an interview with James Dobson, impugned Christians who had invited "these gay children to come into their home and to come into their churches," saying that they had "allowed the enemy to come into our churches." They also must gird their loins anew on this front of the culture war, chase the "the enemy" back into the closet—or eradicate them entirely.

My tribe got to frantic work after the 2015 *Obergefell v. Hodges* Supreme Court case, which gave same-sex couples the right to marry like anyone else. Like the southern bureaucrats who systematically dismantled the racial equality laws of Reconstruction, conservative white evangelicals began hacking away at LGBTQ rights on the state and local levels. The rise of right-wing populism in national politics was a huge opportunity to recapture territory.

It was my tribe working tirelessly to see that, according to the *New York Times*, "nearly every provision that expressed disapproval of homosexuality, same-sex marriage or transgender rights" was included in the 2016 Republican platform. They included much more stringent language than they had even in the party's 2012 platform, even as the slaughter of forty-nine humans in a gay nightclub in Florida was still fresh in the national memory.

My tribe felt a new age of empowerment with a president who promised to fill the courts with reactionary judges. After moving into the White House, his regime did not hesitate to revoke Obama-era protections for LGBTQ people, as well as call for a ban on transgender troops in the military.

The LGBTQ community has seen the Promised Land, and they will not turn around. I am proud to be an ally. I count more than a few members of the LGBTQ community among my loved ones and friends. Some are artists and musicians. Some are social justice activists. Some are married, thanks to *Obergefell v. Hodges.* Some are raising children. I refuse to sit quietly by as my tribe attempts to turn back the clock to a time when these people whom I love were widely reviled, systematically marginalized, and routinely scapegoated, beaten down, and murdered.

The wrangling over what constitutes religious freedom for cake bakers and photographers will continue, but I cannot see the national attitude reverting to biblically literalist positions on human gender and sexuality. I understand that my tribe still sees this issue as an issue of the authority of scripture, and of the God of that scripture, but the cultural paradigm has changed. Heterosexuality is no longer a taken-for-granted dimension of American manhood. Even if they manage to keep their grasp on political power for a time and erase civil rights legislation, they cannot wash the culture clean of this new understanding. They will not turn back the clock, but they will do real harm to people's lives and well-being as they fight what I believe will be inevitable progress.

The Southern Baptists' sit-down with LGBTQ people during the Obama administration might have been a genuine reaching out—or it might have been no more than an attempt to mitigate what they saw at the time as defeat. In 2015, the Southern Baptist Convention adopted a resolution to "stand firm on the Bible's witness on the purposes of marriage, among which are to unite man and woman as one flesh and to secure the basis for the flourishing of human civilization." It also resolved to "love our neighbors and extend respect in Christ's name to all people, including those who may disagree with us about the definition of marriage and the public good."

The real test: will they call off the homophobic pit bulls in their ranks, or will they continue tacitly to condone them, by their silence?

Hey, Teacher, Leave Our Weltanschauung Alone

I N 2006, I SOLD THE Drowsy Poet and went back to school to pursue an MFA in fiction. Having taught high school English in a previous professional life, I looked around Lynchburg and found a job teaching homebound students for the city schools. Because I had worked in juvenile lockups, they gave me the discipline cases—boys, all of them, with cocked heads, crossed arms, wearing sneakers and sneers. I didn't mind. No kid had ever escalated on me without an audience of peers. I taught the boys one-on-one in their homes, most often at a cleared spot at the kitchen table, while a parent tried to stay quiet in another room. I taught during the day, took care of my own children in the evening, and worked on my fiction at night and early in the morning, before going back out to my students.

One day, I had a chance encounter with a dean from Liberty University who had been a regular at my shop. When he'd come in for his coffee, I often stepped out of the kitchen while drying my hands to talk about literature and life with him. We had not seen one another for a while since I sold the shop, and during our conversation he told me of an opening in LU's English department, told me to send my CV straight to him.

The rumor around town was that since Jerry Falwell Sr. had died the previous year, the school was loosening up on its strictures for professors. I had earned the requisite eighteen credit hours in English on top of my MA in religion, and was picking up adjunct work at the community college. But I could not sign LU's doctrinal statement, which the university required. What's more, I had real problems with most of Liberty's social and political positions—plus, my girlfriend at the time (Liz, now my second wife) worried aloud that working there would taint my CV, harm my chances for jobs at other colleges. But this was a full-time teaching position, and I had kids to feed and clothe. I swallowed down real misgivings, said what the hell, and sent the dean my CV.

Several days later, I spent the morning touring Liberty's campus and talking to various members of the administration. Before lunch, my faculty escort dropped me back in the English department for a meet-and-greet. After introductions and small talk, the lone woman in the group of teachers asked if I was ready for "The Inquisition." The other professors laughed.

"What's 'The Inquisition'?" I asked.

"The doctrinal," one of the men said.

On my itinerary was a two-hour block of the afternoon devoted to the "doctrinal." After a pleasant lunch with the dean and a couple of other men, my escort took me to a classroom in Demoss Hall. Three men and one woman sat at a long brown foldout table in the classroom. On the table in front of each of them was a copy of my statement of belief, required since I could not sign their doctrinal statement.

A man with hair cut short as a boot camp recruit took the lead and told me the purpose of the meeting was simply to make sure we were a good fit for one another. He introduced the questioners: he himself taught business; the woman, psychology; one man was from the seminary; another taught biology.

The seminary professor started the questioning by asking about my father. He and Dad were friends; their connection was Appalachian Bible College.

Then he asked, "Does a Muslim go to heaven when he dies?"

I knew the answer he wanted was: no, of course a Muslim does not go to heaven. Instead, I told him I was not qualified to say what the afterlife might be like for a Muslim.

He scowled and wrote.

"How old is the Earth?" the biology professor asked me.

I said I was an English teacher and was happy to defer to geologists on that question. Having grown up in this world, I knew exactly what they wanted me to say, but I did not want to utter an outright lie.

"Would you say it is thousands of years old," he said, "or billions of years old?"

I again played the geologist card. I wanted a full-time teaching gig.

The psychologist asked about the circumstances surrounding my divorce, my present relationship with my ex-wife, and the chances for reconciliation. The man in charge asked me how I planned to "incorporate a Christian worldview" into my teaching. How we had loved talking in seminary about our weltanschauung—our worldview—which we were setting out to defend against the onslaught of secular humanism.

Dad's friend from the seminary grilled me at length on eschatology and showed real frustration that my answers were not Baptist. The biology professor asked me if I thought it was immoral to kill a baboon so a child could have its heart—in order to be sure I believed animals had no rights but existed, along with the entire created world, for the pleasure and benefit of humans.

The Inquisition went on this way for the entire two hours, after which I was escorted back to the dean's office. A stack of books and sample syllabi waited for me. The dean discussed the job with me, quoted a salary figure, and asked if I would accept it. I did. He welcomed me and told me to show up the following Monday for new faculty orientation.

The next day, the dean called and said he had jumped the gun and had to withdraw the offer. "I'm sorry about this," he said. "I think you would have done a great job."

"I'm sorry, too," I said. I was sorry for him: that he had to be the one to call and tell me, and that this had to be what we would think of when we saw one another around town from then on. I was not sorry I didn't get the job. I'd been conflicted about it, and Liz had rightly dreaded the thought of my being sucked back into that world.

No one had asked me about pedagogy beyond the Christian worldview question in the doctrinal, or about teaching English, specifically. No one had observed me teach a class (though, to be fair, it was summer). I had failed the doctrinal, and the committee had torpedoed my employment. The dean told me to apply to teach in Liberty's booming online program—where, apparently, apostates can slip through with relative ease—and sidle into classroom teaching from there. I told him thanks but no thanks, and that was when I finally severed my association with Liberty University forever. I removed the seminary degree from my CV and breathed a sigh of relief.

In 1971, I was a five-year-old boy playing beside the Elk River, while in Lynchburg, Jerry Falwell Sr., with no formal education beyond four years at the then-unaccredited Baptist Bible College, was founding an institution of higher education and ensconcing himself as its chancellor. In 1979, he held up his Bible during a sermon at Thomas Road Baptist Church and explained the educational philosophy of Liberty Baptist College (which became Liberty University in 1984). He said, "We give all kinds of academic freedom, as long as it agrees with this book. If it doesn't, it isn't academic."

His words in this sermon are recorded in *Jerry Falwell: An Unauthorized Profile*. He continued, "I want you having all the academic freedom you want, as long as you wind up saying that the Bible account is true and all others are not."

These are not just the rantings of an ignoramus, a rube. Matthew Avery Sutton writes in *American Apocalypse: A History of Modern Evangelicalism* that conservative white evangelicals "correctly understood that the philosophy at the root of modern university education differed in substantial ways from their own." For example, the evolution-creationism controversy was not about what the scientific evidence bore out. It was about questions at the core of my tribe's identity: "Were humans moral creatures made in the image of God or were they the descendants of soulless animals . . . ? Was the Bible a reliable and eternal source of truth or a flawed product of its times? Was the purpose of education to raise godly children or to expose them to the latest scientific ideas?"

According to Sutton, conservative white evangelicals understood that, according to the secular university's standards of academic freedom, "religion, and Christianity in particular, represented simply another lens through which to view the world rather than the foundation on which to build a holistic education." They knew their weltanschauung could not survive the withering light of science under these circumstances, and they clung to the doctrine of biblical inerrancy for their dear lives.

I can remember hearing pastors and Christian schoolteachers alike say that if our tribe admitted the Bible had a single error, then we could no longer stand firm on any claim it made. It is this doctrine of inerrancy that leads people like Ken Ham to his young-Earth creationism. After a blog post I wrote in 2014 about the debate between Ken Ham and "Science Guy" Bill Nye at Liberty University, I had a brief exchange with a commenter who identified himself as Paul. Though himself a biblical literalist, Paul took issue with my claim that Ken Ham was a biblical literalist, and that biblical literalism was the thick lens to blame for his myopic view of the scientific evidence—Ham said anyone who did not use his literalist lens was not Christian.

For example, the moderator asked each of them, "What would it take to change your mind?"

"Sufficient evidence" was Nye's reply.

Ham responded, "I am a Christian"—which, to him, meant he must take the Bible as authoritative and reject any evidence to the contrary, no matter how strong.

Paul himself turned to arguing in support of biblical literalism, specifically a six-day creation, somewhere between six thousand and ten thousand years ago. Here are some of his comments:

"If you interpret Genesis as figurative, that causes problems with what the Bible says elsewhere (example: Romans 5:12 says that death is a result of sin, but if evolution is true then death existed before Adam and Eve existed) . . . Of course the days in Genesis 1 are 24-hour days. If they weren't, you'd have problems with Exodus 20:11, Exodus 31:17, as well as other verses. So, yes, it is natural to read Genesis 1 as literal 24-hour days . . . Like I said, when Ken Ham responded with 'I'm a Christian,' I think he means that there is no scientific or historical evidence that would contradict the Christian worldview."

To Paul, Ken Ham's position, and the doctrinal statement of Liberty University (indeed, of virtually all conservative white evangelical churches and institutions) making the disparate parts of the Bible support the young-Earth framework, is far more important than dealing honestly with the scientific evidence. If you believe in inerrancy, you must simultaneously do mental gymnastics and hermeneutical geometry to make the evidence fit the texts. There is simply no way to look honestly at scientific evidence on this basis—your purpose for research must be, as Liberty University's Center for Creation Studies website clearly states, "to promote the development of a consistent biblical view of origins in our students." As the twentieth-century philosopher Bertrand Russell wrote of the thirteenth-century Catholic philosopher and theologian Thomas Aquinas: "He is not engaged in an inquiry, the result of which it is impossible to know in advance. Before he begins to philosophize, he already knows the truth; it is declared in the Catholic Faith. If he can find apparently rational arguments for some parts of the faith, so much the better; if he cannot, he need only fall back on revelation. The finding of arguments for a conclusion given in advance is not philosophy, but special pleading."

This is a real problem for those at evangelical colleges whose own intellectual curiosity takes them outside the received doctrines—not just at hardcore fundamentalist schools like Liberty University, but at more intellectually open evangelical colleges like Wheaton. On February 10, 2016, Wheaton College officials and Wheaton professor Larycia Hawkins gave a press conference in which they announced they had mutually agreed to part ways. The school and Dr. Hawkins stated publicly that they were both satisfied with the terms of her departure, but the details remained confidential.

The story behind the press conference was that Wheaton had attempted to fire the political science professor for heresy, maybe even apostasy. Hawkins—the school's first tenured African American female professor—was placed on administrative leave for wearing a hijab in support of Muslims who found themselves under attack from then presidential candidate Donald Trump. According to college officials, the real problem was her claim that Christians and Muslims worship the same God.

This was not the first time Hawkins had landed herself in trouble for thinking out of bounds. According to the *Chicago Tribune*, before this final episode, Wheaton had reprimanded Hawkins three times in the nine years she taught there. She was called out once over a paper on black liberation theology, which one college official thought smacked of Marxism; once over a Facebook photo that put her too close to a gay pride parade; and yet again when she lobbied to diversify the college curriculum and include more inclusive discussions of sexuality.

Wheaton's handling of Hawkins led Peter Conn to publish "The Great Accreditation Farce" in the *Chronicle of Higher Education*. Conn argued that an evangelical college like Wheaton should not be granted accreditation. "Skeptical and unfettered inquiry is the hallmark of American teaching and research," he wrote. "However, such inquiry cannot flourish—in many cases, cannot even survive—inside institutions that erect religious tests for truth." He concluded, "The contradiction is obvious."

Robert P. George makes a tu quoque argument in his book *Conscience and Its Enemies: Confronting the Dogmas of Liberal Secularism*. "We begin to understand the much misunderstood and abused concept of academic freedom," he writes, "when we consider the central importance of the interrogative attitude to the enterprise of liberal-arts learning. The interrogative attitude will flourish only under conditions of freedom." George holds out for "freedom" because it "is as necessary to the intellectual life of man as oxygen is to his bodily life." So far, so good—he decries the loss of academic freedom in higher education. He is not talking about Christian higher education.

George alleges, "The strong leftward tilt and the manifest ideological imbalance at most of our nation's colleges and universities" make it "almost always the case that the victim of the attack is a student, professor, or member of the administrative staff who has dared to write or say something . . . that disputes a politically correct dogma."

He is quick to give religious schools a pass from his list of colleges inimical to the unfettered pursuit of truth: "the legitimate scope of expression is obviously narrower," he writes, "in institutions that are founded on particular religious and moral principles than it is in institutions that proclaim themselves to be nonsectarian and nonpartisan."

When George uses terms like "politically correct," "nonsectarian," "nonpartisan," he is shifting the conversation from academic freedom in scholarship to the realm of political ideology. This shift does just what young-Earth creationists do when they red-herring the conversation from an assessment of factual evidence to a discussion of conflicting worldviews. This is another front in the culture war: they are on God's side, and therefore can never compromise.

My tribe is at the vanguard of this assault on the liberal university. Their influence in the Republican Party has grown ever since the Reagan era, and kicked into high gear over the course of Barack Obama's presidency. Once looking out at the educational establishment from behind wagons circled around biblical inerrancy, they saw new hope. They would use political force to retake institutional ground long ceded to the "politically correct dogma" of the left and the "religions" of secular humanism and science.

In a September 2017 speech at Georgetown University Law Center, then-attorney general Jeff Sessions threw down the gauntlet, saying that freedom "of thought and speech on the American campus are under attack." He claimed the American university "is transforming into an echo chamber of political correctness and homogeneous thought, a shelter for fragile egos." He announced that the US Justice Department would be filing a "statement of interest" in a lawsuit brought against a Georgia college for allegedly infringing on an evangelical Christian's right to proselytize freely.

A Pew survey conducted during the summer of 2017 indicated that 58 percent of Republicans believed colleges and universities were having a negative effect on the way things were going in the United States. The major reason for this opinion was the belief that the university was a liberal hothouse, breeding wild-eyed radicals and silencing conservative voices.

The College Republican National Committee decried "liberal intolerance" on its website, and offered several examples of student protesters demanding that their college bar conservatives, some with controversial views, not just from speaking, but also from the academic conversation altogether. A few examples: Graduating seniors at Notre Dame walked out in protest as Vice President Mike Pence delivered their commencement address. Bethune-Cookman students yelled down Secretary of Education Betsy DeVos as she attempted to deliver her address to them. Student protesters repeatedly shouted down white nationalist Richard Spencer as he attempted to speak at colleges across the nation. Protests devolved into violence when sociologist Charles Murray visited Middlebury College.

First, I do not find it hard to see why students would take umbrage over agitators like Charles Murray. Murray, according to the Southern Poverty Law Center website, believes that "disadvantaged groups are disadvantaged because, on average, they cannot compete with white men, who are intellectually, psychologically and morally superior."

Second, a closer look does not bear out their claims of rampant liberal intolerance. Although incidents of campus protest have sparked a lot of interest, their number is quite small relative to the thousands of guests visiting college campuses, a great many of whom are establishment conservatives. My tribe is not doing battle with liberal intolerance, not really; they are in an epic battle of grand narratives, which cannot coexist.

My tribe fights to restore in higher education a worldview they themselves can never regain, much less foist on the public. If they prevail in the present struggle—I hope neither they nor any other fundamentalist group does, but as I write this, I cannot say they will not—what they erect in the name of Christianity will not be the reestablishment of some beleaguered but intact weltanschauung, not the good "old-time religion." It will be a cartoon drawing of a tree, which they will call the living thing, and demand students water its roots in biology class.

In Mammon We Trust

I AM DRIVING TO WORK. IT is a bright morning in central Virginia, the sun tipping in from over the Blue Ridge Mountains so horizontally that the car's visor only works when I am going downhill. It doesn't matter that much anyway—these Lynchburg roads are so curvy, the sun moves like a blinding cursor on the windows, right to left, up and down. I am on my way to work. I crest the hill and descend toward the community college where I teach English, and bathed in all this fresh sunlight is a vista that fills me with disgust—I could even call it loathing. Twenty years ago, if you looked across the valley, you would have seen rolling Virginia hills, lush and green. Now, the entire horizon has been denuded as completely as a West Virginia strip mine.

Those responsible do not reclaim the destroyed earth, however, or leave it to bleed itself out into creeks and streams. Instead, heavy equipment crawls over it. Construction cranes loom over new buildings in various stages of erection. One building's skeleton this morning, covered by neon-lime insulation panels, appears dangerously nuclear, framed by the natural green of the mountains. A parking garage squats beside a sprawling parking lot, a baseball stadium on one side, a basketball arena under a segmented dome that people in town call the Death Star on the other. A $50 million library named for Jerry Falwell Sr., beside a highway named for Falwell Sr., reportedly has robots to run and fetch your books for you. A football stadium is the linchpin of an empire-builder's hopes—Bill Pennington reports in the *New York Times* that Jerry Falwell Jr. is waving hundreds of millions of dollars from LU's online-school windfall at the NCAA, trying to get his football team into the big league.

Crowning the crowded mess, on a central, obliterated mountaintop is the first-of-its-kind-in-America snowless ski slope. People who have tried it describe it to me as wet white Astroturf, and by my own observation not a single dark human shape has dotted the vast white slope any time I've glanced up there over the past few years. The structure, with its chalet at bottom, stands empty day after day, bringing to mind decrepit 1980s shopping malls or, better, the sad pictures I've seen of abandoned Olympic venues around the world being slowly broken down and slowly overgrown.

To the left of the snowless ski slope is the gigantic circle where the trees have been cleared away for an "LU" large enough to be seen ten miles away, in the town of Forest. I have always called the bald spot on the mountainside "The Wound" because it reminds me of a shaved and bandaged head wound, but people from LU call it "The Monogram." I like what my kids tell me they call it over at E. C. Glass High School: the "Liberty Tramp Stamp." In the valley between the community college and LU, Ward's Road crawls with cars, festers with chain stores, and suffers with strip-mall sprawl.

In 2016, Jerry Falwell Jr.'s plan to build a tower, according to the *Liberty Journal* (which I still receive in the mail), as a "capstone to Liberty's half-billion dollar makeover" was in the news because it would be so close to the regional airport that it might interfere with flights. At 275 feet high, it might briefly sate Falwell's obsession with superlatives by being the "tallest building in Lynchburg," and it would house "the world's largest accredited school for religious studies and ministerial training." The obelisk would be a monument to conservative white evangelical triumphalism—according to the *Liberty Journal*, Independence Tower, now standing, serves to "recognize Liberty's commitment to the uniquely American values of individual liberty, limited government and Judeo-Christian principles." It is also a monument to one man and to his son's personal hubris.

I was a student at Liberty Baptist Theological Seminary in the early 1990s, when Falwell Sr. was hawking a video "documentary" for $43 a pop detailing all the evil deeds of my tribe's then-current enemy, President Bill Clinton. Clinton, this video alleged, was guilty not only of sexual misconduct, but also of money laundering and cocaine smuggling. He was even personally responsible for multiple murders.

Contempt for the president and first lady swirled in thick clouds around Liberty University. My Old Testament professor took a break from classroom instruction one day to tell this joke: "A man walks into a bar and sits down. Hillary Clinton comes on the TV, and he says aloud, 'Now doesn't she look like a horse's behind.' He gets dirty looks from the men in the bar. He sits for a while, and Hillary's picture comes on the TV again. He says, 'If she doesn't look like a horse's behind, I don't know who does.' At this, one of the men stands, walks over, and punches him in the face. Rubbing his jaw, he says, 'I don't get it. This seems like a nice conservative town.' Another man says to him, 'You don't understand. This here is horse country.'"

The hate fest was delectable, but Hillary and her husband were only the latest faces of liberals coming to persecute my tribe. Driving around Lynchburg, I discovered a talk radio host named Rush Limbaugh who ranted against women he called "feminazis" and made fun of Jesse Jackson by derisively mimicking Jackson's speaking voice. More than one car on Liberty's campus was emblazoned with a "Rush is Right" bumper sticker. At LU, Limbaugh was seen as a man out there doing battle on the front lines of the culture war.

I tuned in to his show a few times as I drove around town, and one day, as he extolled the virtues of capitalism, he spoke glowingly of someone named Ayn Rand. How had I missed this Rand person? I jotted down the name and hit the library, which led me into a Rand bender: *Atlas Shrugged, The Fountainhead, We the Living, The Romantic Manifesto.* I devoured a book by her disciple Leonard Peikoff, *Objectivism: The Philosophy of Ayn Rand.*

Rand begins with the idea that existence exists, which is her axiomatic principle, the starting point from which she builds her belief system. From there she is quick to deny the possibility of spiritual reality, much less any kind of god. Eventually she ends in a place where selfishness is a high virtue, altruism a despicable vice, and capitalism the only sane economic system—those who are worthy get rich; those who are poor deserve to be poor.

I had been steeped in right-wing rhetoric my entire life. Now I was studying scripture and theology for myself, and reading a good bit of literature and philosophy on my own outside of class. I was growing, changing. It seemed clear to me that Rand's economics contradicts every principle Jesus preaches in the gospels regarding wealth and care for the poor.

My friend Hiawatha, then the president of the graduate student government, asked me to pen occasional columns so that the graduate school would have a presence in LU's student paper, *The Champion*. My first essay was about this strange phenomenon of turning Christ's message upside down and boldly calling it Christian. I typed the title "Rush Is Not Right" at the top and sent it off. The editor refused to publish it; I refused to write another one. The relationship ended there.

I felt like Biff Loman in Arthur Miller's *Death of a Salesman* after he discovers his father is an adulterer and is spending the family's much-needed money on his mistress. How did my tribe come to this place? To make sense of it, I think it is necessary to understand two conservative white evangelical paths that run parallel for a number of years. The paths are capitalism and the prosperity gospel. It is also impossible to deal with my tribe's economics without a hard look at racial factors.

In *One Nation under God: How Corporate America Invented Christian America*, Kevin Kruse finds the roots of my tribe's current economic values, "not in a spiritual crisis, but rather in the political and economic turmoil of the Great Depression." Industrialists and business leaders met on Park Avenue to plan their fight against the New Deal and figure out how to best preach "the gospel of free enterprise" during the Depression. At this time they were taking a beating as being selfish and predatory, while the Social Gospel—care for the poor and disenfranchised, as Jesus commanded—was ascendant in (at least parts of) Christian America.

These industrialists opposed to the New Deal discovered a preacher named James W. Fifield Jr., who was not a fundamentalist but was an apologist for the fabulously wealthy—and not opposed to grabbing some of that wealth for himself. He pursued millionaires to fill his pews, and lived in a mansion in an exclusive development on Wilshire Boulevard in southern California. According to Kruse, Fifield and his wife "employed a butler, a chauffeur, and a cook, insisting that the household staff was vital in maintaining their 'gracious accommodations' during the depths of the Depression."

Fifield preached Christian libertarianism. He told the millionaires that they were not the greedy ones. They were the makers, and the "New Dealers [the takers] were the ones violating the Ten Commandments." He preached that the federal government was making itself a false idol, "leading Americans to worship it over the Almighty," and that "it caused Americans to covet what the wealthy possessed and want to steal from them." He encouraged the industrialists to recruit preachers who could preach to their congregations that "the welfare state was not a means to implement Christ's teachings about caring for the poor and the needy, but rather a perversion of Christian doctrine." Proper Christianity, he taught, was about saving souls, not taking care of the poor.

The mid-twentieth-century fundamentalist preacher Vance Havner summed up my tribe's two basic assumptions about the poor: "If they had a social gospel in the days of the prodigal son, somebody would have given him a bed and a sandwich and he never would have gone home." The first assumption is that the poor are poor because of their own moral failing. The prodigal son had his chance like everyone else, and he blew it. The second assumption is that the poor need a change of heart, a turn toward God and right living, and not financial help—indeed, help only keeps them from realizing their poverty is their own damn fault.

After Donald Trump dropped out of the 2012 presidential primaries, Jerry Falwell Jr. invited him to deliver a chapel sermon at Liberty University's convocation (not a typical college convocation, but the name for Liberty's thrice-weekly mandatory student church services, once called chapel). After the praise and worship singing, Trump bashed Obama—standard Liberty University fare—and praised the American dollar.

Amy Trent, writing for the *News & Advance*, reported that Trump slipped in some instructions: "I always say don't let people take advantage . . . Get even. And you know, if nothing else, others will see that and they're going to say, 'You know, I'm going to let Jim Smith or Sarah Malone, I'm going to let them alone because they're tough customers.'"

There is no way to spin this so that the advice is not categorically opposed to Jesus's unambiguous command to turn the other cheek and not seek revenge. Following Trump's anti-Christ chapel sermon, Falwell Jr. stood up and revealed his true allegiance. Trump had just instructed all those young "Champions for Christ" to ignore the poor man from Galilee and practice revenge instead. Falwell joked that he wished it were not too late for Trump to get back into the presidential race. It did not seem at the time like even a remote possibility.

Here is the irony for conservative white evangelicals: in allying themselves with big business and wealth, Christian libertarian preachers—James W. Fifield and his conservative white evangelical counterparts—helped erect a Maginot Line against what they saw as godless socialism; at the same time, they cheered and waved flags as the blitzkrieg of godless capitalism swept around their defenses. In the name of Christ, they abandoned the cause of Christ for a culture war based on class and race—on tribalism, which group gets to have the money and the power. If you identify the term "Christian" as did those who coined it to describe the original Christians at Antioch, as people who behave as Jesus Christ behaved, then the political and cultural warfare of the Christian Right is demonstrably unchristian activism.

The responses I get from conservative Christians are telling: "There's nothing wrong with being rich," one family member said to me. Another said, "Are you saying we should take away money from the rich and hand it to the poor?"

Jerry Falwell Jr. is rich and getting richer. He inherited the college presidency from his father in 2007, and by 2016, according to a report in the *Chronicle of Higher Education*, Falwell Jr. was pulling down a $926,634 salary, making him the second-highest-paid private college president in Virginia. Mark Demoss, chair of the executive committee of Liberty's board of trustees, said in an interview in 2015 (before he disagreed with Falwell Jr. over Donald Trump and was removed from the LU board) that Falwell's exorbitant salary was justified because Liberty University "brings in about $250 million annually in profit."

Ironically, a big chunk of that cash came from the hated tax-and-spend big federal government. Mary Beth Marklein, writing for *USA Today* in 2013, reported that big government money gushing into Liberty's coffers at the time amounted to an estimated annual "$775 million in federal aid, including loans and grants."

In April 2017, LU's website bragged about the installation of "a carillon of 25 bells weighing approximately 8 tons," at the top of the obelisk. Seventeen stories tall, with 409 steps from top to bottom, the tower is indeed "the tallest building in Lynchburg." Added to the eyesores of the Liberty Tramp Stamp and ski slope, Independence Tower, the monument to a reenergized conservative white, male, evangelical triumphalism, rises, a giant phallus, into the Lynchburg sky. According to the website, the tower now houses, in addition to the Liberty University School of Divinity, the Center for Apologetics & Cultural Engagement.

This is nothing new, of course. Of Christians amassing wealth and political power in the name of Jesus, Nietzsche's criticism in *The Antichrist* appears more apt than ever: "with impudent selfishness they always wanted only their own advantage; out of the opposite of the evangel the church was constructed . . . one would look in vain for a greater example of world-historical irony."

Suffer Not a Woman

DEBBIE LIVED ACROSS THE OLD railroad, stripped of its track and by then a rutted and potholed dirt road in front of Elkview Baptist. The house was tall and decrepit. In my memory, it was the gray-brown of wood left unpainted for long years. The top and bottom floor both had sloping porches across the front. It caught fire one Sunday night while we were in church, hopelessly disrupted the service, and then burned to the ground. Debbie was probably five or six years older than I was and had an older brother named Fred. Other members of the household hover in my memory, but they were older still. One, whose name I don't remember, would eventually hang himself in jail.

The only actual interaction I remember having with Debbie was when I was in grade school. She and Fred were down in the wooded bottom before the church bought it, and they cleared the trees with hatchets and rope, to build a cabin. Vaughn and I were down there playing as well, and Debbie and Fred tied us up in their little cabin clearing and told us they were holding us hostage and planned to chop us up—she held her hatchet close to my face—if our parents did not pay a ransom.

They were not going to harm us, and we knew it, but for a couple of grade-school boys, it was just real enough to take on the air of high adventure. As we negotiated with them, I worked myself free of my bonds, and when they were both at the far end of their clearing, hacking at tree limbs for their cabin, I broke free and bolted through the trees. I ran up to our house and into the kitchen, where I grabbed a handful of candy corn shaped like jack-o-lanterns and ran back through the woods. I offered the candy as ransom for Vaughn, and, having lost interest in us anyway, they accepted my offer. I saw Debbie around for a number of years to come, but I cannot remember ever speaking to her directly again.

What was remarkable about Debbie in Elkview in the 1970s was her masculinity that was far beyond acceptably tomboyish. In high school, she wore boys' jeans and shirts, and did not bother with hairstyle and makeup as the other girls did. She walked like a boy, too—not like any boy, but with a tight-jawed, John Wayne–style swagger. Eventually she had a Jeep CJ with a removable top, and wore a wallet on a chain.

One Sunday night, Debbie showed up for a church service. She drove up in her Jeep with another butch girl, and the two of them walked into the church, and sat through my father's nervous sermon, their chins high and defiant. When the service was over, they stood and walked back out. People were astounded at their gall. Even as a kid, I understood that they were giving notice: we are not playing by your gender rules anymore.

We had a man named Walt in the church who was a nurse. Walt was a big man with a wife and kids, not effeminate like Mr. Eagle down at the elementary school, but Walt's career choice was still considered questionable. One way you could tell was that church members invariably included his gender as a modifyier when mentioning his profession: he was always referred to as a "male nurse," never just a "nurse." He was in a field still considered the realm of women—the intimate caretaking so much like mothering; why was he not a doctor? People offered justifications: he was good at it; it paid decent money; anyway, who says nursing is a woman's field? The same went for Mr. Schaffer, who sometimes made delicious biscuits for potluck dinners; everyone was sure to add to their praise of his cooking the fact that he'd been a cook in the US Navy. Debbie's gender transgressions were beyond justification. An aura of scandal hovered around her.

In *Redeeming America: Piety and Politics in the New Christian Right*, Michael Lienesch relates how Phyllis Schlafly laid the blame for "the disease called women's liberation" at the feet of Eve. "The woman in the Garden of Eden freely decided to tamper with God's order and ignore His rules," Schlafly wrote. "Sin thus entered the world, bringing fear, sickness, pain, anger, hatred, danger, violence, and all varieties of ugliness." Women were not only intellectually inferior, but when they stepped out of their God-ordained role, they were also dangerous. They caused the ruination of men, and ultimately the downfall of society.

Though the issue was not new, it appeared to be growing more heated. Robert Self writes in *All in the Family*, "Between 1973 and 1980—in the era of the ERA, *Roe v. Wade* and gay rights—evangelicals, led by right-wing fundamentalists, raised the specter of family breakdown as national ruination." Southern Baptist preacher James Robison blamed the US slide into destruction on "feminists, lesbians and gay men, psychologists, and the Supreme Court." Beverly LaHaye wrote that feminism was "more than an illness . . . It is a philosophy of death . . . [Feminists are] self-destructive . . . and are trying to bring about the death of an entire civilization as well."

Jerry Falwell Sr. warned in his 1980 jeremiad *Listen, America* that feminists "are prohomosexual and lesbian." Members of the LGBTQ community and feminists were lumped together because they all challenged the God-ordained order of family and gender roles. Granted, a certain amount of what my tribe considered manly traits could be admired in a woman—assertiveness, bravery, strength, perseverance in the face of hardship—because it seemed natural that a woman might aspire to be like a man. We knew from 1 Corinthians 11:14 that it was shameful for a man to have long hair like a woman, and so at Elk Valley Christian School, boys' hair had to be off the ears and off the collar, a strictly enforced policy. Girls could wear their hair that short if they wanted to.

There were limits to the way a girl presented herself physically, though, as well as to the control she should have over her own sexuality and reproduction, her professional options, and the way she could live in the world generally. These limits were inviolable because God ordained them in scripture. Robert Self again: "Biblical teachings, evangelicals insisted, made the family rather than the individual, the irreducible unit of social organization. Families were governed by a patriarchal father (in God's image) whose role as breadwinner and disciplinarian was balanced by the nurturing and spiritual figure of the mother. Gender roles were ordained and fixed and not subject to human reimagining."

My mother was a stay-at-home mom, in theory. She did work in the church office next door, which was acceptable. A wife working outside the home was fine under the authority of the husband.

Feminist Gloria Steinem and other women's libbers might have had other ideas, but in my tribe, a woman knew her place. Steven P. Miller writes in *The Age of Evangelicalism: America's Born-Again Years* that Marabel Morgan, in her wildly popular book *The Total Woman*, published in 1973, "offered a 'biblically based argument for submitting to husbands,' called herself 'a wife and mother first and foremost,' and argued that married women should, if possible, stay at home while their children were young."

Given that the patriarchal family unit is the bedrock of society, everything depends on maintaining the man's authority in the home, in the church, and in society. Paul tells Timothy that women are to "learn in silence, with all subjugation," and that he should "suffer not a woman to teach, or usurp authority over a man." He instructs the Corinthians that women are to "keep silence in the churches, for it is not permitted unto them to speak."

Things were this way not only because God had commanded it in scripture—though that certainly would have been sufficient reason—but also because he had created them differently, male and female. Men had a certain set of strengths and weaknesses, and women had another set—mostly weaknesses—and their strengths were best revealed in chastity, nurturing, and obedience. If a woman tried to step outside of her station, only trouble could follow because it was unnatural and, more important, because it angered God and invited his wrath.

Women should be under the authority of men, as my tribe sees it, because they are intellectually inferior and prone to think with their heart instead of their head, which leads to poor decisions. In his article "Are You Looking at Me?," science writer Matthew Hutson notes, "In most cases, thinking of a person as a body does not lead to objectification in a literal sense, in which the person becomes an object. Rather, [the woman] is dehumanized . . . becomes a sensitive beast." This explanation is as good as any I've seen for the view of women in my tribe—if man is the rational animal, woman is the emotional one.

It was a given that women were sensitive beasts, weak creatures unable to think straight when they got emotional. I heard more than one preacher claim the serpent approached Eve in the garden because he knew that she, being a woman, would be easy to trip up. Eve, whom John Milton referred to as "our credulous Mother," let the serpent flatter her and appeal to her vanity, where Adam would have been wise to the serpent's wiles. Women were to be watched, it appeared self-evident; they should be controlled, shielded from important decisions.

In 2014, a friend who had been raised in my tribe told me her preacher father had recently admonished her brother, who was having marriage problems, to control his wife. Men, her dad counseled, "were made by God to be the lords of this earth." He said, "Your wife needs you . . . she needs your lordship to deal with her emotions." When I was single and young, and would join groups of friends at restaurants and bars, more than once, I joined the other guys in chuckling at how the girls had to go chattering to the restroom all together—not once in those times did it occur to me to question why they did not go alone. In the ignorance of my privilege, I thought girls were just silly like that.

In *American Apocalypse: A History of Modern Evangelicalism*, Matthew Avery Sutton quotes one of turn-of-the-twentieth-century evangelist Billy Sunday's sermons: "The average little frizzle-headed, fudge-eating, ragtime flapper who can't turn a battercake without spattering up the kitchen, knows more about devilment than her grandmother did when she was 75 years old." It was clear: women stayed in their place, or they ended up causing trouble. Sunday concluded, "Yes sir, woman is the battleground of the universe." Sutton observes that "fundamentalist leaders almost always blamed women rather than men for the nation's supposed sexual decline."

To my tribe it was clear that God ordained the rules to keep in check the innate dangerous characteristics of femininity. My mother regarded my first serious girlfriend as a danger to my eternal soul. I met her just as my Elkview Baptist youth group's rock and roll tape-burning revival had used up its emotional steam, and all of us teenagers were looking away from the church to our various other interests again. Although I was a lusty seventeen-year-old boy, to my mother this girl was the cause of my obvious backsliding.

This young woman and I dated for a couple of years. We had a pregnancy scare, about which she wrote me a long and heartfelt letter, which Mom found in my room and read. Outraged that the girl had caused me to fall into sexual sin, Mom issued me an ultimatum: if I did not break up with the little tramp, Mom would go tell her parents we were having sex. I refused. I truly loved this girl in my teenage-boy way, and what's more, I was ready to stand up to the moral bullying of my parents—at least, I was ready to try. The girl and I went ourselves and informed her parents we were sexually active, taking away my mother's blackmail power. Her parents demanded she start taking birth control and said nothing else about it, as far as I knew.

In my family's Baptist home, it was a raging scandal. Proverbs 7 warns the young man not to fall into the trap of a seductive woman lest he be led by her to destruction like an "ox to slaughter." Matthew Avery Sutton relates how the twentieth-century evangelist Bob Jones Sr. said in a sermon, "I have ceased to hope for men to live pure until women dress modestly. God will hold you women accountable for the downfall of thousands of men." Not even the preacher could withstand the seductress. In *The Act of Marriage*, Tim and Beverly LaHaye warn women to avoid "scanty dress." They explain that if women understood the psychic damage "their indecent exposure causes the average man, many of them would dress more modestly." If immodest dress was too much, then parking with a boy in a car . . . well.

After Mom tried to save me from damnation by blackmailing me into breaking up with my girlfriend, Dad said to me, "If girls were as loose when I was young as they are now, I probably would have gotten in trouble, too." Women were assumed to be intellectually inferior, but they were still expected to be morally superior, the guardians of purity. The ones who refused to do this were dangerous, indeed.

When my father was in his eighties and my mother had developed Alzheimer's, he still refused to ride alone in a car with her dearest friend, Sharron. In 2017 it was considered newsworthy that Vice President Mike Pence, a conservative white Catholic, followed the "Billy Graham Rule"—no eating alone with a woman other than his wife, no meeting alone with a woman other than his wife, and no attending events without his wife where there would be both women and alcohol.

Many people came to Pence's defense, citing the nobility of his efforts to shield himself from temptation. This sheds light on a paradox in their thinking: women, weak and inferior as they are, wield a power so great no man can ever be truly sure he will be able to resist. (The rule has the added benefit of excluding women from professional spaces where they do not "belong" in the first place.)

Actually, it is even worse than that. Evil women who intentionally seduce men are not the only sexual danger—any woman who has a body is potentially just as dangerous, because her body inflames lust in men. Tim LaHaye explains in *How to Be Happy Though Married* that men are sexual aggressors by nature due to their "constant production of sperm and seminal fluid." He writes that the male drive for sexual satisfaction is "almost volcanic in its latent ability to erupt at the slightest provocation." The message: Women, do not cause the slightest provocation, or you'll get what you deserve.

By this thinking, sin and death entered the world because of woman. Woman has caused the downfall of man since Eve caused Adam's damnation. She wields a power over him that he cannot resist. John Milton's Adam tells Eve the "Enemie hath beguil'd thee . . . and mee with thee hath ruined" because "with thee my resolution is to Die; How can I live without thee . . ." In his book *A Man's Touch: Stepping into the Shoes Only a Dad Can Fill*, Baptist preacher Charles Stanley writes that Eve has Adam so much under her control that all she has to say to him is "Have a bite." What else could he do? Dante places lust at the very top of purgatory, right below the entry into Paradise, for a reason: it is a sin, okay, but a perfectly understandable one, not so bad. Who can blame a hapless man when a woman has captured him with her feminine ways?

What of the man who is so spiritually strong that he can withstand her temptations? What if Mike Pence were to dine alone with a woman not his wife and she tried to seduce him, and he, having read his Bible and prayed that morning, was able to flee the temptation, and she accused him falsely of sexual misconduct? He is still not out of danger, woman being not only silly and seductive, but also sinister in her deceitfulness.

Rebecca Solnit's "Cassandra among the Creeps" deals with the disbelief of women's claims, particularly in the realm of sexual violence.

She writes, "credibility is such a foundational power . . . and women are so often accused of being categorically lacking in this department." When a woman speaks up about male misconduct, "especially if it has to do with sex, the response will question not just the facts of her assertion but her capacity to speak and her right to do so." Solnit goes on to explain how Freud discredited the women he interviewed when what they told him was too damning of men. Instead, he wrote off their stories as dreams born of a secret wish to be ravished. Senator Arlen Specter, participating in the humiliation of Anita Hill, proposed that she "imagined or fantasized Judge Thomas saying the things she has charged him with."

When allegations surfaced that Roy Moore had sexually molested a teenage girl years ago and had made a habit of dating high school girls while he was in his thirties, conservatives rushed to his defense, even using the story of Joseph and Mary (Mary was much younger than Joseph) to justify their continued support of the right-wing firebrand. Jerry Falwell Jr. said, "It comes down to a question who is more credible in the eyes of the voters—the candidate or the accuser." In an email to Religious News Service, Falwell Jr. continued to defend Moore, writing, "The same thing happened to President Trump a few weeks before his election last year, except it was several women making allegations. He denied that any of them were true and the American people believed him and elected him the 45th president of the United States." Falwell insinuated that it was better to believe a pathological liar and sexual predator than to trust a woman. That women are not just deceitful, they are disgusting, something about them is fundamentally unclean.

My tribe's woman problem goes all the way back to Leviticus 15, where we find that God hates menstrual blood so much he declares women who are having their period spiritually unclean. When Donald Trump said of Meghan Kelly in disgust, "blood coming out of her . . . wherever," he was speaking the language of my tribe's (mostly) unspoken mythology.

Women were also viewed as the property of men. A man's wealth could be measured, in part, by how many women he had collected. Solomon had seven hundred wives and three hundred concubines. A bride who turned out not to be a virgin was to be stoned to death, according to Deuteronomy 22, and only virgins should be taken as war booty, and the used women put to death—it's worth noting that girls were ready to be married off when they started menstruating, so these war prizes were likely rather young girls. Think about it. One man's penis had the power to change a woman from a cherished prize to an animal worth no more than death.

The Levitical laws no longer apply, members of my tribe say. We are under a new dispensation—or a new covenant, for the reformed-leaning tribe members. However, as Paul explains to the Corinthians, "For a man . . . is the image and glory of God: but the woman is the glory of the man. For the man is not of the woman: but the woman of the man." As man is to God, so woman is to man. Her existence is onto-logically less than man's, and she is forever and unchangeably, by God's declaration and her own feminine characteristics, in a subcategory. The very essence of her existence is in relation to man as her superior.

Sometimes keeping a woman where she belongs requires a little violence. One of Jerry Falwell Sr.'s standard jokes was that he never considered divorcing his wife, but he had thought of murder a few times. In *The Book of Jerry Falwell*, Susan Friend Harding comments on one such time, when he was speaking to a church full of preach-ers: "the anger and the threat of force here were ironic, but still served as little reminders of men's ostensible physical authority, their 'power-in-reserve.'" "More unambiguously," Harding elaborates, "this flash of rhetorical violence revealed to whom the entire joke about his mar-riage was addressed. It was addressed to men. In this way it not only upheld public male authority, it enacted it . . . Women were meant to overhear them."

To paraphrase Margaret Atwood: Men are afraid women will laugh at them; women are afraid men will kill them. In 1996, Mary Dick-son published "A Woman's Worst Nightmare" on Blue Ridge PBS. In it, she noted the difference between a man's worst nightmare regard-ing women—the case of a woman falsely accusing men of rape had re-cently been in the news—and a woman's worst nightmare about men. "I don't mean to underplay men's fears or this woman's damaging ac-cusations," Dickson wrote, "but what this story underscored for me was the very different way that men and women perceive their own safety." She described another news item she saw the same week as the false allegation story: "A woman was jogging at 5:45 A.M. in a suburban neighborhood when a man grabbed her, dragged her behind a cement wall, repeatedly banged her head into the wall, and brutally raped her."

As women are standing up more often and speaking out, things appear to be changing in the culture at large. Not so among my tribe. Reporting for the *New York Times* in 2014, Richard Pérez-Peña reveals the results of an independent report by Godly Response to Abuse in the Christian Environment (GRACE), giving a glimpse into this aspect of my tribe's mythology. GRACE's investigation had determined that "officials at Bob Jones University told sexual assault victims that they were to blame for their abuse, and to not report it to the police because doing so would damage their families, churches and the university." In the same year, stories broke about similar institutional behavior at Pensacola Christian College and evangelical Patrick Henry College in Virginia. When an authoritarian pastor wolf-prowls among his flock in conservative evangelical churches, it often remains an open secret in the pews.

When the tape of presidential candidate Donald Trump bragging about sexually assaulting women leaked on October 7, 2016, Falwell Jr. redoubled his support for the sexual predator. When even Trump's own voice saying he could "grab [women] by the pussy" whenever he felt like it failed to shake his support among conservative white evangelicals, Falwell said, "And I'm glad to see that."

In May 2016, Baylor athletic director Ian McCaw left the Baptist school amid controversy over his handling of what a lawsuit alleges were fifty-two rapes between 2011 and 2014. Also in 2016, Adam Kilgore penned the *Washington Post* article "Liberty University's Hiring of Ex-Baylor AD Sends a Chilling Message about Sexual Assault." Kilgore reported that an independent investigation concluded that McCaw's tenure over the athletics programs exhibited "a failure to identify and respond to a pattern of sexual violence by a football player, to take action in response to reports of a sexual assault by multiple football players, and to take action in response to a report of dating violence." When Waco police offered to hush up an assault case, McCaw's response was, "That would be great if they kept it quiet!"

With dreams of Baylor-like football success, and unconcerned about McCaw's ignominious departure from the school, Falwell Jr. snapped him up for Liberty University's athletics program.

In February 2017, President Trump appointed Falwell Jr. to a higher education task force. One of Falwell's stated goals for the task force was "to cut university regulations, including rules on dealing with campus sexual assault."

You could imagine a university president wanting to tighten the rules in order to ensure the safety of young women in his care—especially if he knew of at least one case in which a man who eluded justice at his school went on to even greater sexual violence.

In 2002, a young woman attending Liberty University came forward accusing football player Jesse Matthew of rape. It became a question of consent—he said she had wanted it; she said she had not. There were no witnesses. The woman faced the almost impossible ordeal of proving Matthew had raped her, and, as so often happens, she gave up. "Liberty would not say if Matthew was expelled," according to a report on local CBS-6 news, but "non-marital sexual relations that would 'undermine the Christian identity or faith mission of the University,' are considered a violation of the personal code of honor." Matthew did leave LU. The young woman's allegations fell silent.

From Liberty, Matthew went to Christopher Newport University where, in 2003, another young woman accused him of sexual assault. It is not clear how CNU handled the case. Matthew quit the football team and dropped out of school the following week. That accusation faded to silence as well.

In March 2016, Jesse Matthew pleaded guilty to two counts of murder and two counts of abduction with intent to defile, and there are still multiple unsolved cases thought to be his doing. The young women he raped and murdered, Hannah Graham and Morgan Harrington, remain as smiling, silent photographs on their parents' walls. Silence, too, from Falwell Jr., who felt no need, in the midst of his vociferous defense of the sexual predator who became president, to speak on the horrific crimes committed by a man who had escaped accountability at Liberty University.

In December 2017, the satirical web journal the *Onion*, ran the headline "Trump Dismisses Accusers as Women." Like all good satire, the *Onion* article elicits not a gut-busting laugh of hilarity but a groaning laugh of recognition. While Trump was dismissing all of his accusers as women, and calling the tape of his bragging about sexual assault no more than "locker-room talk," I saw an interview with a middle-aged white evangelical couple explaining how they could still support him. The man said, with a slight shrug, "So he likes women. I like women too." A dark look passed across his wife's face as he said this, but she instantly regained composure and smiled at the camera. It might not be as explicit as their defense of young-Earth creationism, but misogyny is every bit as much at the heart of my tribe's mythology.

Social justice activist Jim Wallis calls racism "America's original sin," and he is right. Would it not be correct to say *man's* original sin is misogyny—expressed structurally in patriarchy, justified and perpetuated by religious doctrines penned and codified by men? To give women equal power and equal voice, can we reform it incrementally, or, since this is the foundation of our entire culture, would we have to tear the whole thing down and rebuild?

A Life among Guns

ONE MORNING IN OCTOBER 2015, I descend a flight of stairs at work, having just heard on the news how a man in Oregon shot up a classroom at Umpqua Community College and killed eight of his classmates and the professor. I have just driven in to work after making lunches for my kids and seeing them out the door for their day. At the door, I kissed Grace on the head as she hugged me goodbye, and reminded her that Asher, already on her way to the car, was staying late for rehearsal. Could I come give her, Grace, a ride home?

The Umpqua shooter was on academic probation, the news report stated. He owed the college money. In front of me on the stairs is a colleague with some students, one of whom I recognize as a student of mine. The professor's hair is short on the sides and long on top with floppy bangs wet-combed back, in the current hipster style known as the undercut, minus the beard. From where I stand, I can see that the wisps of long hair only half-cover his balding crown.

The student we share is a freshman, a young man with black hair that hangs to his shoulders. Today he wears a black tee shirt with "Metallica" arced over the picture of a skeletal figure glowing in an electric chair. He is a bright kid, ready to speak, eager to prove himself.

"At the end of the day," he says to my colleague, "we are all children of Kant."

The professor begins his response, but a girl climbing the steps toward me steals my attention. She is one of my students as well, and she is looking down at an essay. Not even glancing up to notice me, or anyone else around her, she says to her friend, "Eighty-two. *Not bad.*"

It was August 1, 1966, a little over one month before my birth, when a man named Charles Whitman climbed a tower at a college in Texas and started picking off students with his rifle. When I was in Marine Corps boot camp nineteen years later, my drill instructor bragged that Whitman had learned his marksmanship on that very Parris Island rifle range.

Twelve died at Columbine High School in 1999. Thirty-three, including the shooter, died in the Virginia Tech shooting of 2007. Almost thirty died at Sandy Hook Elementary School in 2012. In 2015, Dylan Roof gunned down nine Charlestonians at their Bible study because they were black. The 2016 Pulse nightclub shooting left forty-nine dead. The Las Vegas music festival shooting left fifty-eight people dead. There are many other mass shootings—they have grown so common they churn through the news cycle with barely a ripple—but these are the ones that spring readily to mind.

The response to these mass shootings by state legislatures across the nation has been to make guns more accessible—by their reckoning, more guns equals less gun violence. Those who have legal access to guns in some states now include the mentally ill, men under protective orders because they beat their wives, and people too blind to drive. No shit. Look it up. Several states are currently trying to remove age restrictions so children can pack heat. Idaho, Utah, Colorado, and Texas have made it illegal for a college professor to declare her own classroom a gun-free zone. The University of Houston's faculty senate recently sent out a list of things teachers should do to avoid getting themselves shot. One was "avoid provocative statements."

I follow the flow of students down that hallway and peel away into my classroom. I set down my notes and stand at a tall desk beside the whiteboard, annoyed that someone has swiped all the dry-erase markers yet again. Students filter in and stare silently at their phones. The community college shooting still fresh in my mind, I consider what I would do if someone appeared in that back doorway and started spraying us with bullets. I glance down for something to throw. Beside the computer keyboard is a white coffee mug filled with paper clips and one tangled, black USB cable.

I go into a daydream in which I grab the mug and throw it with the excellent accuracy of a hobbit, hit the gun—no, hit the shooter in the eye. While the shooter is stunned, I pull up the removable top of the wooden lectern and rush him, reach him before he can raise his barrel. I bench-press the lectern into him and smash him against the wall, giving my students time to subdue him, wrest away his gun. In my daydream no one dies.

I was aware of a number of people who did shoot someone, or who were shot by someone. I never saw the gun that sent a bullet through my Uncle Harold's brain. The story I remembered from childhood was that he'd gotten in a fight with one of his drinking buddies, and the man, as they say in West Virginia, had killed him dead. I asked my Uncle Bert about it not long ago, and he told me they never found out who shot Harold, but they suspected it was a woman with whom he shared a child, and an ongoing feud.

I had toy guns when I was a boy, as most boys in the late 1960s and early 1970s did: metal guns that popped tiny smoking explosions from red caps, the air filling with the smell of burnt powder. Plastic guns, too, sold in a pack with handcuffs and a hollow plastic billy club. Colorful space guns that sparked inside when you cranked the cold tin trigger. In my memory, the gun that killed Uncle Harold was a pistol, but I have no way of knowing.

We drove from Elkview to Delbarton for the funeral. My grandmother's house was at the bottom of a deep gulch in coal country, and we drove through a low-flowing creek to reach it. There we met up with my mother's family and drove back through the low creek, out to the paved road, and on to the funeral home. Inside, I stood facing the casket beside my Uncle David. He turned his head my way, ducking in his chin at the same time. His eyes closed tight, and his beard-rough mouth formed a snarling silent roar, teeth bared like a dog biting at a flea on his shoulder. He brought up his hand and quickly covered the shame of his grief.

My mother did not cry at all that I saw. On the way home, she sat staring out the front windshield as Dad did his preacher thing on the evils of demon drink. The dead man was my mother's brother, and here was my brother beside me, my sister, too. I could not make sense of it. It was too big and too dark. I did not know my uncle. Today, the only thing I remember about him is that I think he was a coal miner, he was a mean drunk, and someone shot him dead in a parking lot.

When I was in fourth grade, my brother and I watched out the window of our bedroom as two men fought viciously on the snow-packed parking lot of the church where our father preached. At some point, one of the men held the other at bay with a shotgun barrel to his chest. We knew what shotguns did to squirrel bodies. We watched, waiting for the blast, the blood, the falling body.

No gun blast, but one of the men did beat the other down with the butt of the gun. Before evening service, my brother and I walked to the spot of the fight and stared down at the blood—in my memory it bloomed, suspended in the ice like silt clouds made by crawdads down at the creek in summer.

Not long after that fight, my cousin Beckham shot and killed his next-door neighbor. I remember that it was a shotgun he used, but I never saw that gun, either, so I can't say for sure. Beckham and his neighbor were fighting, and the neighbor went into his house for a gun. As he returned with it, Beckham shot him dead in the front yard.

"If he had waited until the man came into his house," one of the adults said. "If he had waited, it would've been self-defense." Beckham sat in prison for two years and then went back to his life as a poor workingman in southern West Virginia, or Missouri or Ohio, I'm not sure.

An old man in my father's church named Mr. Riddle had a gun collection that was the envy of men up and down the Elk River. He gave Dad a 20-gauge, pump-action shotgun. We had other guns, but that one was my favorite. It was a heavy gun, the black metal of its barrel thick and solid like no BB gun I'd seen. The woodgrain swirls on the stock were wavy like the rings of oil on water. More than once, pellets from another shotgun showered through the leaves onto me as I hiked through the woods with that gun. I never knew whether to call out because the shooter didn't know I was there, or haul ass because he did know. A couple of times I aimed back along the trajectory of the pellets and fired a return volley.

One night during my senior year of high school, I rode into Charleston with friends to party. While I was gone, a guy from my school named Butch called the house asking for me. Mom told him I was out. He said he had a gun, and he was on his way out to find me and shoot me. When I returned home late, I was surprised to find her in the kitchen waiting for me. I turned to hide the beer on my breath.

"Butch called," she said.

"Butch?" I asked, adding his last name to be sure, because Butch and I exchanged nods in the hall between classes, but we did not call one another on the phone.

Mom told me he was out to shoot me. She asked why. I told her truthfully that it was about a girl. She nodded. Was she scared? She didn't show it, but my mother was ever the stone-faced stoic. Anyway, isn't that what the men in her family did, shoot and get shot?

Once, at a keg party, I watched a guy aim a loaded 12-gauge shotgun at my brother's chest and demand he chug his cupful of beer. The boy was just showing off. It was his house and he was bored with quarter-bounce.

The police held me at gunpoint three times in my youth. Twice because I was a rowdy young buck who foolishly believed an old redneck who had said, "Every boy should get thrown in jail at least once before he settles down." The third time the police pulled their guns on me was a legitimate case of mistaken identity. Wrong place, wrong time. Vaughn and I were in the front of our roommate's car, and I was driving. Our roommate was slobbering drunk in the back seat. When the police officers trained their guns on us from both sides of the car, our drunk roommate yelled at them, cursed them, as Vaughn and I sat up front trying not to piss ourselves. The officers had more urgent concerns that night than a drunk college boy. If I had not been a white boy in very white places, I would likely right now be many years dead.

My second year of college, I was out with two friends, Doug and Angie. We were in Angie's Honda Civic. She was from Milton, West Virginia; the men of her family worked on the railroads and tucked their flannel shirts into their blue jeans. Her older brother had given her a .22 pistol, and she kept it loaded and wrapped in a dishtowel under the passenger seat of her Civic. It was silver, and the fat handgrip was bigger than the snub barrel. It looked like a toy.

While Angie was inside her friend's apartment, Doug and I stayed in the parking lot to flirt with some girls who were on the building's front stoop. It was all harmless fun until four or five guys rolled up, jumped from the car, and confronted us—the girls, it turned out, were their girlfriends. Doug pulled out a pocketknife, and the guys all laughed at him and started walking toward us. I unwrapped the pistol and held it up so they could all get a good look. Having never seen a gun so small, I feared they might think it was a toy, but they were city boys and they knew damn well what it was.

As I watched those boys fall over themselves and run for their car, I understood anew how a gun could make you feel powerful. Beside me, Doug laughed and hollered as he paced off his adrenaline. I stared in wonder at the little gun in my open palm.

The semester after I brandished the pistol, I joined the Marine Corps Reserves. I ended up in the Gulf War, the one called Desert Storm. I tromped across miles of sand with a black M-16 strapped to my body. I imagined battle scenarios, wondered if I would shoot a fleeing enemy. After struggling with why I was there in the first place, I decided I would indeed shoot anyone who was shooting at me. It never came to that. We arrived at the war four days late, and every Iraqi we encountered was already captured or dead. At war's end, I turned my rifle back in, having fired not a single round.

Looking back over life with guns in my tribe, it occurs to me that I was always in the most danger from gun violence at home among my own. All the big guns of our military, the vast array of arms we had amassed, we watched those create a pillar of fire moving before us, raining down explosive, bloody death on anyone in our path. Occasionally an enemy round would slip through and kill one of us, but the truth is, I was in no more danger there—and possibly less—than I was with the good, but sometimes unpredictable, guys with guns back home.

Sometime around 1996 I took my nephew Jesse to the firing range at Kanawha State Forest to teach him how to shoot. I have not fired a weapon since then. It was not by choice. I was simply not around guns anymore.

On December 4, 2015, NPR published a web article titled "A Tally of Mass Shootings in the U.S." The report stated there are around eleven thousand gun homicides per year in the United States. While that sounded like a lot, the number of gun deaths was actually declining year by year.

My son, Evan, told me he'd read a book arguing that advanced societies are becoming less, not more violent. He said maybe, hopefully, it indicates we are evolving out of the survival need for violence. Is he right? According to the Pew Research Center, the number of gun homicides per year is half what it was in 1993 (but the trend has reversed since then, and gun deaths are again on the rise in the United States). The horror of mass shootings continues. Why? Is it growing pains, the lashing out of those being left behind by a society maturing into a new, peaceful incarnation? I tend to be less sanguine than Evan about human nature.

I'd like to think he is right. I'd like to think humanity is getting better, and we should take comfort from this long view, ignore the alarmist evening news. Except that I'm a father. I send my kids into the world knowing that some pissed-off man might randomly gun them down. It is unlikely, I know, statistically speaking. It is so rare as to say it never happens—except when it does happen. My own children have not grown up with guns the way I did. It was not a choice I made because I am against guns. I simply never enjoyed hunting, and I don't see bagging your first kill as a rite of passage. We scouted out the best school playgrounds. We played tennis and basketball. We played music—actual instruments—and acted in plays. We watched *Lost* together as a family, and *Glee*. We played Scrabble and The Settlers of Catan.

Fire drills are a standard part of the school experience. When I taught in Ohio years ago, I experienced tornado drills for the first time. In an op-ed for the *Los Angeles Times*, Lisa Lewis explains how new active shooter drills work at her son's high school. "A Level One is when an active shooter is in the town or city; a Level Two is when the shooter is in the neighborhood; and a Level Three is when the shooter is actually on campus." When her son's school went on lockdown one day, he downplayed her mother's concern by saying, "It was just a Level One." The problem with active shooter drills, according to Lewis, is not only that they "scare the hell out of the community," but, more tragically, that they "normalize atrocities."

At the beginning of every semester, faculty and staff at my school sit through a video about what to do when an active shooter shows up on campus. The video instructs us to react in this order: run if you can; if you can't run, hide; if you can't run, and you can't hide, fight with all the violence you can muster.

Someone has invented bulletproof backpacks for kids to get small behind, and bulletproof rest-time blankets so smaller children have somewhere to hunker. Children are now anxious about going off to school in the morning, but not just because they didn't finish their homework—they are afraid they might be shot dead at their desks.

I descended into my basement writing room yesterday morning and jumped straight to procrastinating. Among the items on my news feed was a report that yet another man had shot up a bunch of people he barely knew. The headline sufficed; I did not click on the article. I opened a story I was writing, and I sat staring at four pictures pinned to the cabinets in front of my writing table.

One picture is a charcoal drawing of a human skull, my memento mori to help me focus on the work at hand every morning. The other three pictures are curling snapshots from years ago, hanging by a single thumbtack each.

The bottom one is of Evan and Asher playing at Kanawha State Forest when Evan was not yet three and Asher was just walking. In the photo, the two of them are in front of a picnic shelter, and they are smudged and smeared, face to bare feet, with the dirt of outdoor play. They are both squatting at a dog's metal water bowl, splashing in it with sticks.

The middle photo is of Evan on my sister's lap. They both face the camera. Alma has her arms wrapped around Evan's chest, and their faces are side by side—that they are related is clear by their sharp Sizemore chins.

The top photograph was taken by an employee at The Drowsy Poet. All three of the kids are at the sandwich board "helping" me prep for lunch. Asher and Grace are mangling mushrooms with serrated spreaders, and have stopped working to mug for the photo. Grace still has a fat toddler head. Evan is slicing cucumber disks with a 10-inch bread knife. He does not have time for the camera. Ever the serious little man, Evan watches his work, holding his fingers so carefully, his mouth tight in concentration. His bangs splash open at his cowlick.

Evan, Asher, and Grace are all young adults now. They are out of my sight and, except for advice and financial help, out of my care. They move through a conservative Christian South where, more and more, I see white men walking around packing heat. The owner of the Irish pub where I met friends for a beer the other night swept the sidewalk in front of his bar while wearing a black 9-mm pistol shoved into the waistband of his jeans above his ass crack, outside his shirt, for all to see.

Are guns really such a danger, though? I sent my kids out among cars as much as I did among guns, and I know, according to the statistics, cars kill far more young people in the United States than guns do. Cars are convenient in their growing into a meaningful adulthood, though—unless they move to a larger city with better public transportation, or maybe out into the woods to take up homesteading. Cars are getting safer every year, to the benefit of all of us who drive. The automotive industry is also relatively well regulated. Guns could be getting safer, too—the technology is available—even though the one thing they are designed to do is take life, but the National Rifle Association drowns out common sense with its shouting about the Second Amendment. In her essay "Fear," published in the September 2015 *New York Review of Books*, Marilynne Robinson writes that the reason many Americans are obsessed with maintaining unrestricted access to guns is because "America is full of fear."

Why is the NRA so full of fear? Why is it so hell-bent on keeping assault rifles, designed for nothing other than killing as many humans as possible as fast as possible, available to angry, fearful—and often crazy—people? Where is the great threat?

If we take the organization's 2017 recruitment videos seriously, the threat is liberals and their president (Obama), and people protesting the Trump regime. The NRA intends to "save our country and our freedom" by fighting "this violence of [liberal] lies with the clenched fist of truth."

Under the Trump administration, just as racists are taking off their masks and stepping into public view, so, too, the NRA is revealing its true raison d'être. A video posted to the NRA website on August 3, 2017, shows an NRA spokesperson declaring the organization a militia to fight the enemies of Donald Trump—generally the free press, the *New York Times* in particular. She says, "We the people have had it. We've had it with your narratives, your propaganda, your fake news. We've had it with your constant protection of your Democrat overlords . . . and we've had it with your pretentious, tone deaf assertion that you are in any way truth or fact-based journalism." She tells the *Times*, "Consider this the shot across your proverbial bow . . . in short, we're coming for you." They are not just arming to stand their ground against black boys with Sprite and Skittles; they are preparing for war against a free press that calls them out on it.

The last time I visited Elkview Baptist Church, one of my mother's friends, a grandmother named Sue, stood before me in the Fisher Fellowship Hall and discussed the pistol she was buying to pack in her purse. My father said he'd like to see a Muslim terrorist come through the doors of Elkview Baptist Church because they'd get shot to pieces by the people there to praise Jesus—remember, the "turn the other cheek" guy, the one who founded the "God hath not given us the spirit of fear" religion?

On the last day of March 2016, the *Huffington Post* reported on the "Mississippi Church Protection Act." The act, passed by the Mississippi senate, would give churches the right to form armed militias, and would "exempt them from legal action if they use their weapons" to protect the congregation. Liberty University started allowing concealed carrying of firearms on campus in 2016, and students may keep guns in their dorm rooms. Liberty also built a multimillion-dollar gun range, in part to demonstrate, one interviewee told the local news admiringly, Falwell Jr.'s "commitment to the Second Amendment."

My tribe's obsession with the Second Amendment arises from the same impulse as their Trump support did—white cultural anxiety, the fear that brown people are growing in number and are coming to do white people harm. This also explains the fact that mass shooters are overwhelmingly white men.

I know the Baptists up the Elk River are locked and loaded in the church sanctuary, peeking warily at the world outside their doors, under the church motto, "The Church That Cares." They have gone mad with fear. Do not go in there and make any sudden moves, especially if you don't look sufficiently white evangelical. Mom's friend might whip that gun out of her purse and shoot you dead.

I spent my childhood and youth around violence and guns. Men pulled them on one another in anger and sometimes pulled the trigger. Sometimes they do use the guns in legitimate self-defense. In 2015, the pharmacist in the Good Family Pharmacy in Pinch, West Virginia, across the river from Elkview, shot and killed a would-be armed robber. The robber's surname was one I remembered from my childhood in Elkview; he was most likely a local boy addicted to methamphetamine or opioids. The mass shootings continue. The gunmen remain overwhelmingly male and white. It is a sad irony that my tribe arm themselves to stand their ground against nonwhite invaders from outside their walls, while all this time the call has been coming from inside the house.

Atheists, Demons, and Saints

"Y OU DON'T BELIEVE IN GOD?" I ask Liz one evening in 2006.
At that time, we had only been dating for a few months. It was a legitimate question in Lynchburg, a city with a higher percentage of Baptists than Salt Lake City has of Mormons. Finding an atheist around here who was open and vocal about it was like spotting Bigfoot—their children were harassed at school, told they were going to burn in hell forever.

We approach the one traffic light between Randolph College, where she works, and her apartment. It is dark out, almost ten at night. She hunches forward in the dull orange glow of the streetlight, hugging her coat closed. She turns her head down in the cold car as if laying it on an airplane pillow. The bottom half of her face disappears into shadow.

"Is that a problem?" she asks.

"No," I say. "Should it be?"

We had just attended a Richard Dawkins lecture, billed as a discussion of his book *The God Delusion*. Dawkins did not argue against belief in the supernatural, or some kind of divine reality. He had his rifle loaded for a single deity. Dawkins, a small, mild-looking man with a smooth British accent and ironic tone, stood at the lectern with a wry smirk and insulted Yahweh, the God of the Hebrew scriptures and the Christian Old Testament. He ended his rollicking diatribe by calling God a "megalomaniacal meany."

Dawkins knew he was only a few short miles from Liberty University, where all philosophy courses are necessarily in some way apologetics classes. He also had to have seen the rows of Liberty students—entire classes, it looked like, complete with teachers—unmistakable around town in their unofficial J.Crew uniforms. They took notes feverishly, flipped through books and Bibles, scrambled and shoved to line up at the microphone when he finally opened the floor for questions.

For over an hour Liz and I watched students hasten up and down the aisles, flipping through their apologetics books, coached and goaded by their teachers. Eventually Dawkins stopped impugning the character of God and instead insulted the intelligence of anyone ignorant enough to associate with "that school on the other side of town." Undaunted, the kids were still lining up to get at him as Liz and I slipped out.

Several times in the evening, I noticed Liz nodding her agreement with Dawkins, and so I asked her about her unbelief.

I had just that week pulled the twentieth-century French writer Albert Camus's novel *The Plague* off my shelf to reread. Having moved much further away from my evangelical upbringing than I was the first time I read the book, I was having a far different experience with the book this time around. At the time of the Dawkins lecture, this question was already in my mind: Why do I have such an affinity for Dr. Bernard Rieux, the protagonist of this novel? Why do I feel a sense of communion with Camus?

In *The Plague*, Camus's protagonist Dr. Rieux echoes Ivan Karamazov's bitter cry "Until my dying day I shall refuse to love a scheme of things in which children are put to torture." The disease ravaging Oran is no respecter of persons, and it tortures and destroys innocent children along with everyone else. Dr. Rieux concludes that, "since the order of the world [God created] is shaped by death, mightn't it be better for God if we refuse to believe in him?"

As a youth, I heard more than one preacher quote Ivan Karamazov—or more likely, quote from a book of sermon illustrations—that "if God is dead all things are possible," then point to what they saw as the moral freefall of American culture as proof of what happens when people stop believing in God. Ivan's denial is not the triumphal shout of a man wanting to misbehave with impunity. He knows that having a God who gives meaning and purpose to life is far more appealing than being able to sin without fear of punishment. Ivan is crying out that if God does not exist, all manner of horrors are possible. Dr. Rieux looks around, sees that all manner of horrors are not just possible, but pervasive. Unbelief is simply the reasonable assumption that if there really were an all-powerful God who was all-good as well, the world would not be as it undeniably is.

In 2006, Liz worked with the Lynchburg Neighborhood Development Foundation, a local organization whose work is among the poorest neighborhoods. The LNDF is no more, but Liz still does her work in these neighborhoods. She champions service learning, teaching her students by taking them out to work with community leaders on real economic problems. Her students must come face to face with the disenfranchised, know them as individuals, and treat them with dignity and respect. In the summer of 2019, she was instrumental in bringing the first CDF Freedom School to Lynchburg and worked tirelessly to help get it up and running.

In *The Plague*, Dr. Rieux pushes himself to his physical limits combating the epidemic. He labors with the devotion of Mother Teresa to alleviate suffering. He says that though he does not believe there is any ultimate meaning in it, he does feel he is on the right road in fighting against creation as he finds it, and he believes all humans should "struggle with all our might against death." Why does Dr. Rieux persist in doing good when he believes there is no God, and without God there is no meaning to any of it?

A phrase I heard repeatedly in my Baptist youth was the Psalmist's admonition, "The fool hath said in his heart, 'There is no God . . .'" The early-twentieth-century Spanish Basque writer Miguel De Unamuno, in his classic *Tragic Sense of Life*, writes that it is a true statement, but adds that we must make a clear distinction between head and heart in order to understand the Psalmist. Someone who denies God in her *head* because of despair at not finding Him is not the fool described in this psalm. For Unamuno, a righteous and good person can reasonably conclude that God does not exist. The fool is someone who concludes in his *heart* there is no God, and that therefore he is free to do as he pleases without regard for others.

To my tribe, the atheist—the one who says in her head there is no God—is the fool. Unamuno discards this interpretation, I think rightly so. A character in *The Plague* wonders aloud to Dr. Rieux if it is possible to be a saint without believing in God. Unamuno's answer is an unequivocal yes. His head-heart distinction goes down easily for a boy who grew up in the Baptist church where preachers spoke of people missing heaven by 18 inches—"the distance from your head to your heart." What is astonishing here is the radical change of paradigm, the reversal of categories.

I recently reread Dostoyevsky's novel *Demons*. When I pulled it off the shelf, the top was fuzzy with a fine coat of dust, and brushing it off sent me into a sneezing fit. The jacket on my copy is pale yellow and on the front, in black and red, rising from what could be a grave or a building or a pile of lumber, are five men, one in a stovepipe hat, and the others in what look like imperial officers' hats. Their faces are distorted, eyes tight, teeth bared in rage and madness. They are the possessed.

You might find this novel under the title *The Possessed* or *The Devils* (which is a more literal translation). Translators Richard Pevear and Larissa Volokhonsky chose *Demons* because they wanted the title to be a clear reflection of what they saw as Dostoyevsky's main concern: his focus is not so much the possessed, the men, but the demons that possess them.

As a young man, Dostoyevsky renounced his Russian Orthodoxy for atheist materialism. "I have acquired the truth," Pevear, in the foreword, quotes his telling another writer, "and in the words God and religion I see darkness, obscurity, chains, and the knout."

When Dostoyevsky wrote *Demons*, he had suffered a great deal, and he had become a Slavophil, a reactionary standing against the progressive liberal ideas of the West, and a Russian nationalist who believed their Orthodox Church was the bearer of the one true God. In the novel, a character confronts another with words that echo Dostoevsky's own famous assertion: "But wasn't it you who told me that if someone proved to you mathematically that the truth is outside of Christ, you would better agree to stay with Christ than with the truth?" By the time he wrote *Demons*, Dostoyevsky was boldly making this proclamation—he had essentially become a fundamentalist.

In *Demons*, the devils that possess the young men are ideas, "idea-demons"—rationalism, positivism, nihilism, materialism, socialism—and at the heart of all of them, Dostoyevsky places a kind of idea-Satan: atheism. Atheism gives birth to the ideas that possess us and make us commit evil deeds.

What does Jesus have to say? Nicodemus comes to him by night (John 3:1–21), and Jesus tells him, "Ye must be born again." I know the story well. Going back to it, I notice the shift in Jesus's own words from belief to actions: "For everyone that doeth evil hateth the light . . . But he that doeth truth cometh to the light, that his deeds may be made manifest, that they are wrought of God."

I look back over the rest of the red-lettered portions of the New Testament, to remind myself what Jesus has to say. In Matthew 21, he gives the parable of the two sons. The one son says to his father, "Yes, I will do as you ask," then does not; the other son says to his father, "No, I will not," but then goes and does as he is asked. Jesus is quite clear that the son who says the no and does the yes is the truly righteous son. In light of Unamuno's words, quoted above, this parable could be seen as Jesus's approval of a man like Dr. Bernard Rieux. What should make prosperous evangelicals a little uncomfortable here is that once the dust settles on these new categories, if a good atheist is in, who might be left out?

Flip forward to Matthew 25: Jesus is quite clear about who is blessed and who is damned. He does not mention a conversion experience of any kind, or the keeping of rules. He does not mention belief at all. He declares blessing on those who struggle against real human suffering, and reserves damnation for those who do not.

Liz considers all this talk about blessing and damnation so much nonsense, and so would Dr. Rieux; however, Camus has embodied in Rieux what he considers to be the only course of action for one who longs for meaning yet sees none: hold out for meaning in the face of all evidence to the contrary by sheer force of will.

How, though? Act. Your action itself will create meaning. But not just any act will suffice. In his 1957 Nobel banquet speech, Camus called his listeners to "fight openly against the instinct of death at work in our history." In an absurd world void of meaning, is it not just as much nonsense to call for action of any kind, much less one kind over another?

Camus refuses to descend into nihilism, and he refuses to take the stoic's way—those whom Jonathan Swift lampoons as ones who would rather cut off their feet than admit they need shoes. Camus has the integrity to admit his heart longs for "the absolute and for unity," even while his head denies they exist. He will not lop off his desire in order to deny its source. His position is not so far removed from Unamuno's "transcendental pessimism." After conceding that the evidence of reason is not enough in itself to justify belief, Unamuno concludes, "Let life be lived in such a way, with such dedication to goodness and the highest values that if, after all, it is annihilation which finally awaits us, that will be injustice."

We awaken and discover ourselves dropped into existence in medias res, and it is impossible to lift ourselves above the flow of history to get a universal perspective. Like it or not, we are contingent; we owe our existence to something other than ourselves. Whatever we believe that something to be, we feel ambivalent toward it.

Even though we might debate the concept of evil, there is no disputing the existence of suffering. Our natural reaction to senseless suffering—the suffering of innocent children—is anguish and rage. Our options are clear. If we act, our actions create meaning. The way I see it, being contingent as we are—and therefore being incapable of creating anything ex nihilo—the meaning we create with our actions is in reality a reaching down and drawing on a deep well of meaning, an absolute, a unity, an Ultimate Other—call it God, if you like. The ability to create meaning through moral action is what Nikolai Berdyaev calls the "freedom of the spirit," and he points to this as clear evidence that humanity bears the divine image.

More nonsense, Liz would say. I think of Rieux, who appeals to me so much because, regardless of belief or lack of it, he is good. He acts as if there were a deeper meaning to it all, even if his reason tells him it makes no logical sense. Liz is good also, good and compassionate and fair. She lives her life according to a high moral code, and she is interested in justice, but not without mercy. She does not need a WWJD bracelet on her arm to remind her to do the right thing; she has the moral compass in her heart.

As I read *Demons* again, I couldn't help but think about the state of our nation, the increasingly angry rhetoric in public life, the inescapable swirl of religion and politics, rhetoric of persecution and resistance—even revolution. We appear to be hurtling headlong into what, in the words of the old Chinese curse, will be ever more "interesting times."

Dostoyevsky foresaw his country's dark destiny, but his identification of atheism as the source of the problem was as mistaken then as it is today. When I was a young Baptist, Dostoevsky's labeling of atheism as the idea-Satan birthing the demons of socialism and communism made perfect sense to me. Now, not so much. Atheists can be found everywhere on the political spectrum, just like believers. They are also every bit as capable of being kind and thoughtful human beings—in my experience, they are generally *more* kind and thoughtful than believers.

I am old enough to remember the specter of Soviet communism, but communism itself is not a demon-idea. Remember, when the Bolsheviks rolled into power, thousands of Tolstoyans across Russia were endeavoring to live out a communalism based on the teachings of the New Testament—the Soviet communists purged them from the landscape during forced collectivization. Feminism is not an idea-demon, nor is LGBTQ rights, or social justice, or secular humanism, or evolution. Atheism is certainly not the idea-Satan.

If the root of idea-demons, the idea-Satan, is not atheism, what is it? What would an idea-demon even be? To my thinking, an idea-demon is any idea that degrades and dehumanizes those who are not like us. An idea-demon is any that makes scapegoats of the weak and defenseless; it is any idea that favors sending fleeing refugees back to certain misery and possible death instead of taking them in and caring for them; it is any idea that allies itself with the rich and powerful against the dispossessed. Nationalism is an idea-demon. White supremacy is an idea-demon. Racism, xenophobia, misogyny, homophobia, transphobia, religious triumphalism—all idea-demons.

When I asked Liz on the way home from the Dawkins lecture if she believed in God, she eventually said, "I don't see enough evidence to justify belief."

Fair enough.

I do see enough evidence to justify at least leaving the question open. As much as my head might spin in disbelief, confident unbelief is simply not a living option. Yet the senseless suffering of innocents fills me with anguished questions for and about God. I struggle with the problem of evil—the honest apologist knows in her heart that no answer puts this question to rest.

What do I do, then? I strive to act with integrity, to live simply, to take only what I need. I endeavor to deal compassionately with others, try to understand them as human beings with dreams and desires no less important than my own for their being different. Like Bernard Rieux, I fight against injustice and suffering; like Albert Camus, I fight against "the instinct of death at work in our history."

This is what Liz does as well. In spite of what I'd grown up hearing about atheists, I was comfortable with her answer that night in the car. While our heads might disagree, our hearts do not. I see that it is possible for one to stand on the side of belief, and another to stand on the side of unbelief. They can stand on either side and yet look in the same direction. They can look with a deep and human longing, a longing that rises from a shared place where sorrow and comfort mingle and flow in a deep love for the world and people in it, regardless of belief or lack thereof. They can stand on either side, and yet be so close that the most natural thing in the world to do is join hands.

Conclusion

Goodbye, My Tribe

IT IS SUNDAY MORNING, AND I sit in the sunroom at back of the house where Liz, the kids, and I have lived since Liz and I married in 2008. Three walls of windows make it almost as if I am outside in the tree-shaded backyard—the morning view without the morning chill. It is the gray time before sunrise; the raccoons, skunks, and foxes have slipped back into hiding, and the squirrels and birds have yet to emerge. Everything is motionless, or so it feels—the spot where I sit is actually spinning at almost 900 miles per hour around the axis of Earth, which itself corkscrews at 66,000 miles per hour to keep its orbit around the sun, which is hurtling through space at 43,000 miles per hour.

Outside, the gray lightens toward blue, and inside the house is dark and silent, ensconced in sleep. Our black German Spitz, Sergeant Pepper, has relocated from his new bed in the living room to the stone tiles here beside me, where, with a couple of soft groans, he has rejoined the house's deep slumber. Since the death of our older dog, Molly Bea, he has started following us around, preferring to do his sleeping close to some living body, even if his only options now are human.

After her stroke on election night 2016, Molly Bea held on until February 2017, when euthanasia was the only humane option remaining. Liz sat on the kitchen floor and held her head so she could, weak and blind as she was, lap strawberry yogurt from its white plastic cup one last time. I carried her to the car, and we drove to the vet. Liz sat on the floor with her there as well, and I sat on a bench beside them. The doctor shaved Bea's leg, put her to sleep with a sedative, and then injected the pentobarbital that stopped her heart.

"Take as long as you need," the vet said as he stood up from administering the fatal dose. He quietly left the room. We were there with Molly Bea; she was there with us, and she was gone. Liz stroked her fur a little longer, and we went home.

I am not sure why, but the black buzzards who winter here did not fly away for the summer in 2017. They took up residence not on the old Victorian house but on a power line tower on Burnt Bridge Road. They were there yesterday as I drove by, and I guess they are there right now, preparing their awkward wings to lumber out for last night's roadkill deer, squirrel, and groundhog. When Liz and I take evening walks, we sometimes walk by their tower; the grass and sidewalk are scattered with long black feathers, and the buzzards sit silently together up there, maybe watching us, maybe not concerned in the least about us.

Outside the sunroom's French door, across the yard and over the trees, the sky lightens slowly in the east. From this perspective, it would be easy to imagine the Earth flat at the center of the universe, and the sun arcing across the sky every day, as ordered by God. Just the other day, I saw an article by David Kelly in the *Los Angeles Times* about the growing number of people who mistrust science so much they've gone back to believing the Earth is flat. It has apparently burgeoned into a bona fide movement. Most scientists do not even bother arguing with them, their belief in a flat, stationary Earth is so ludicrous.

David Falk, assistant professor of astronomy at Los Angeles Valley College, does argue with them. He told Kelly the flat-Earth movement "is a scary thing." He said, "The danger isn't that people don't believe the Earth is round, it's the lack of scientific literacy." Here, as with my tribe's young-Earth creationism, the science is irrelevant—they are not interacting in the realm of actual science, but in the realm of competing grand narratives. When asked why scientists would want to deceive so many people, a leader in the flat-Earth movement responded, "They want to dissuade you from the idea of a God . . . They want us to think that we aren't special, but we are."

A C-SPAN video of vice-presidential candidate Mike Pence made the rounds of social media during the 2016 presidential race. In it,

Pence, then a representative from Indiana, repeatedly derides evolution in a speech on the floor of congress as "just a theory." Using the lay definition of *theory* (a hunch or intuitive notion) and not its scientific definition (an explanation of phenomena substantiated by sufficient and typical experiment, testing, and evidence), Pence is unhappy that the "theory" of evolution is taught in school textbooks as "fact." New scientific discoveries, he says, are making it necessary to change all the schoolbooks to discard the old fact of evolution and teach a "new fact."

He was advocating the teaching not of new facts, but the *alternative facts* of creationism, "the theory," according to Pence, "that was believed in by every signer of the Declaration of Independence." As if this were a sound reason to believe in young-Earth creationism; remember, the signers of the Declaration of Independence also believed in humoral physiology and bloodletting. Pence then turns to scripture and preaches his view of science: "The Bible tells us God created man in His own image, male and female he created them." As a flat-Earther interviewed for the *Los Angeles Times* article said, "They want us to think that we aren't special, but we are."

Is it possible to revive a dead mythology? I have seen several articles in the past couple of years about Iceland's reestablishment of Norse paganism a thousand years after the missionary Thangbrand arrived from Norway with the gospel of Jesus (and a spear for those who refused to accept that good news). It appears to be catching on.

A few months ago, Alma, Vaughn, and I converged in Charleston to pack up our parents' household. We had found them a small, one-story place near Elkview Baptist, where Dad still teaches a class on Wednesday nights and Mom walks around getting hugs from the ladies. We arrived to find that church members had already done the bulk of the work. I packed up my father's office, leafing through books and papers as I did so. Apparently, the newest church charter and by-laws no longer prohibit the use or participation in the sale of "alcohol as a beverage," a huge concession to younger church members, I would guess. Beyond that, as far as I can tell it's the same harsh fundamentalism of my childhood and youth. Yet I no longer see this belief system as a benign religion about a God who "so loved the world."

Dad comments on the infrequency of our trips to visit him and Mom. I sometimes feel guilty about it, but we exist in two opposed realities. When I step into their house now, for an instant Dad and I stand like enemies who have stumbled upon one another in the forest and must choose to raise a weapon or dive for cover. Alma, Vaughn, and I always were something like strangers who lived in close proximity to him, so there is not even an intimate history into which we can retreat for common sanctuary. His insistence on our tribe's "truth" is intransigent, and his call to proclaim it is inviolable.

Alma and I drive up the river to their new place. We sit in their new living room. WVU football is on the TV. The space between Dad's chair and the couch where I sit is a chasm too wide to span. Over it roils a turbulence that distorts all but the low-flying words—we make small talk, communicate nothing meaningful at all. Apparently, Mom's dementia has now reached a stage where she is perpetually angry with Dad when they are alone; she is happy to see her children when we visit, seems to know that she knows us, but has no idea who we are to her. This nuclear family's story is very close to its conclusion. Only the final chapter remains.

There is a saying in my tribe: If you feel far away from God, guess who moved. I know this gulf exists because I am the one who moved. For my own sake and that of my children, I am thankful I did move. As this last, sad chapter of Mom and Dad's family story comes to a close, I imagine I will enter a conservative white evangelical church two more times. After that, I will bid a final goodbye to my tribe.

I am already thankful I got away from the worst of it before raising my children. Evan graduated from college in 2018 and went to Sierra Leone with the Peace Corps. I am thankful he does not feel that being a white American man affords him an elevated status that must be defended against women and people of color. I am thankful that, as a reader and freethinker, he does not lie awake at night terrified that his musings might take him out of bounds, might land him in an eternal burning hell.

Grace is in college now, and her interests lean toward male-dominated fields. She will be pushing into a strong cultural headwind,

but at least we did not teach her that a woman's place is in subservi-
ence to a man. She has white conservative evangelicals in her circle of
friends, and it appears that they, like many other Trump supporters,
become more defiant in their support of him as his criminality and
malignant narcissism become more obvious. Gracie loves her friends
and she wants the conflict to go away. I know I run the risk of alien-
ating her if I am not careful, if she sees my strong opinions as judgment of the friends whom she chooses. Yet I hope, as she spends time
with them, their pernicious ideas do not seep in and take root.

Asher is finishing up at the University of North Carolina at Greens-
boro's school of music. She is also living publicly as a trans woman.
As I write this, states are acknowledging advances in our understanding of gender and sexuality; they are taking steps to allow people like
my daughter fully to take part in life as they are, things like adding
nonbinary gender options for drivers' licenses and ID cards. I hope
things for Asher and other trans people are changing for the better in
the culture overall. I hope she can walk into an America ever more accepting of her, and less dangerous to her.

Grace's Trump-supporting friends, the flat-Earthers, and Mike
Pence sermonizing to Congress spring from the human desire to feel
special in the world. If being softly and tenderly created by the all-
powerful God of the universe who even now looks over you in love
and longing doesn't make you feel special, what would?

However, that need not translate to a literalist reading of the Bible
and an adherence to a dead tribal mythology. The neopaganism now
revived in Iceland, for example, is not the same religion killed off by
the missionary Thangbrand. Hilmar Örn Hilmarsson, high priest of
Ásatrúarfélagið, an association that promotes faith in the Norse gods,
explained in a *Guardian* interview, "I don't believe anyone believes in
a one-eyed man who is riding about on a horse with eight feet. We see
the stories as poetic metaphors and a manifestation of the forces of
nature and human psychology."

Myth as poetic metaphor. Of course.

I am not antireligion in general or anti-Christian specifically—I
know and admire some devout believers, even count them as friends—
but I am antifundamentalist. I know my tribe will never stop fighting

to take dominion of the culture and enshrine their deeply held religious beliefs into law. I will oppose them for the rest of my life.

It took me years to claw my way free. I am thankful my children will not have to do the same. I am thankful my tribe's pernicious notions are not the lens through which Evan, Asher, and Grace view the world, not the metric by which they measure the worth and worthiness of others or themselves. My children are young people, and they are facing away from my tribe's harsh and fearful mythology. They are at the mouth of a dark cave, looking out onto the world. Sure, it is a world of danger and uncertainty, but it is also a world of bright possibility. I see the goodness in them, and I do not despair. They are the true substance of things hoped for, the evidence of things not seen.

Works Cited

Addley, Esther. "Back for Thor: How Iceland Is Reconnecting with Its Pagan Past." *The Guardian*, February 6, 2015. https://www.theguardian.com/world/2015/feb/06/back-for-thor-iceland-reconnectinbg-pagan-past.

Anderson, Nick. "Virginia's Liberty Transforms into Evangelical Mega-University." *Washington Post*, March 4, 2013. https://www.washingtonpost.com/local/education/virginias-liberty-transforms-into-evangelical-mega-university/2013/03/04/931cb116-7d09-11e2-9a75-dab0201670da_story.html.

Atwood, Margaret. *Second Words: Selected Critical Prose*. Toronto: House of Anansi Press Limited, 1982.

Bajekal, Naina. "Silent Night: The Story of the World War I Christmas Truce of 1914." *Time*, December 24, 2014. http://time.com/3643889/christmas-truce-1914/.

Baldwin, James. *Notes of a Native Son*. Boston: Beacon Press, 1955.

Ball, Molly. "Is the Most Powerful Conservative in America Losing His Edge?" *The Atlantic*, January–February 2015. https://www.theatlantic.com/magazine/archive/2015/01/is-the-most-powerful-conservative-in-america-losing-his-edge/383503/.

The Bee Gees. "Too Much Heaven." In *Spirits Having Flown*. Issued by RSO, 1979; reissued by Reprise, 2006. Record album.

Berdyaev, Nicolas. *Freedom and the Spirit*. Brooklyn: Semantron Press, 2009.

Berkhof, Louis. *Systematic Theology*. Grand Rapids, MI: Eerdmans Publishing, 1996.

Bivins, Jason C. *Religion of Fear: The Politics of Horror in Conservative Evangelicalism*. New York: Oxford University Press, 2008.

Blumenthal, Max. "Agent of Intolerance." *The Nation*, May 16, 2007. https://www.thenation.com/article/agent-intolerance/.

Botton, Alain de. "Atheists, Believers & the Secular." by Anne Strainchamps. Wisconsin Public Radio, April 21, 2015. https://www.wpr.org/listen/746441.

———. *Religion for Atheists: A Non-Believer's Guide to the Use of Religion*. New York: Vintage Books, 2012.

Bowler, Kate. *Blessed: A History of the American Prosperity Gospel*. New York: Oxford University Press, 2013.

Bryan, Alix, Melissa Hipolit, and CNN Wire. "Victim Allegedly Raped by Jesse Matthew at Liberty Never Filed Charge." WTVR, September 26, 2014. https://wtvr.com/2014/09/25victim-allegedly-raped-by-jesse-matthew-at-liberty-dropped-charge/.

Bryan, Alix, and Chelsea Rarrick. "Sexual Assault Filed against Jesse Matthew at Christopher Newport University in 2003." WTVR, October 1, 2014. https://wtvr.com/2014/10/01/sexual-assault-filed-against-jesse-matthew-at-christopher-newport-university-in-2003/.

Brydum, Sunnivie. "Scott Lively's Crimes against Humanity Aren't Conservative Christian Outliers." Religion Dispatches, June 6, 2017. http://religiondispatches.org/scott-livelys-crimes-against-humanity-arent-conservative-christian-outliers/.

Burgess, Anthony. *A Clockwork Orange.* New York: W. W. Norton, 1962.

Bush, George H. W. "George H. W. Bush's State of the Union Address, Envisioning One Thousand Points of Light." Infoplease, January 29, 1991. https://www.infoplease.com/history-and-government/famous-presidential-speeches/george-h-w-bushs-state-union-address.

Bush, George W. "Text of President Bush's 2003 State of the Union Address." *Washington Post,* January 28, 2003. http://www.washingtonpost.com/wp-srv/onpolitics/transcripts/bushtext_012803.html.

Campbell, Joseph. *The Hero with a Thousand Faces.* 3rd ed. Novato, CA: New World Library, 2008.

Camus, Albert. "Albert Camus Banquet Speech," December 10, 1957, the City Hall in Stockholm, Sweden. https://www.nobelprize.org/prizes/literature/1957/camus/speech/.

———. *The Plague.* New York: Vintage Books, 1991.

Chick, Jack. "The Gay Blade." Chick Publications, n.d. Accessed May 2, 2019. https://www.chick.com/products/tract?stk=0084.

CNN. "Viral NRA Ad Sparks Controversy." YouTube, June 30, 2017. https://youtu.be/9bBQq9GdeKI.

Coates, Ta-Nehisi. "The Case for Reparations." *The Atlantic,* June 2014. https://www.theatlantic.com/magazine/archive/2014/06/the-case-for-reparations/361631/.

Cogley, John. "God Is Dead." *New York Times,* January 9, 1966.

Cohen, Leonard. *You Want It Darker.* Columbia Records Group, 2016. CD.

College Republican National Committee. "When Liberal Intolerance Crowds Out Debate on College Campuses." CRNC, March 11, 2017. http://www.crnc.org/liberal-intoleranceo-crowds-debate-college-campuses/.

Conn, Peter. "The Great Accreditation Farce." *Chronicle of Higher Education,* June 20, 2014. https://www.chronicle.com/article/The-Great-Accreditation-Farce/147425.

Davidson, Michael Scott. "PCC Grapples with Sex Abuse Allegations in Viral Blog Post." *Pensacola News Journal,* April 20, 2014. https://www.pnj.com/story/news/2014/04/21/pcc-grapples-with-sex-abuse-allegations-in-viral-blog-post/ 7952657/.

Dawkins, Richard. *The God Delusion.* New York: Houghton Mifflin, 2006.

Dickson, Mary. "A Woman's Worst Nightmare." *No Safe Place,* 1996. https://www.pbs.org/kued/nosafeplace/articles/nightmare.html.

Dorr, Lawrence. *A Bearer of Divine Revelation.* Grand Rapids, MI: Eerdmans Publishing, 2003.

Dostoevsky, Fyodor. *The Brothers Karamazov.* New York: Bantam Dell, 1984.
———. *Crime and Punishment: Norton Critical Edition.* New York: W. W. Norton, 2019.
———. *Demons.* New York: Alfred A. Knopf, 1994.
———. *The Idiot.* New York: Vintage Classics, 2001.
Falwell, Jerry. *Falwell: An Autobiography.* New York: Tab Books, 1996.
———. *Listen, America!* New York: Bantam Books, 1980.
Feldman, Kiera. "Sexual Assault at God's Harvard." *New Republic,*
    February 17, 2014. https://newrepublic.com/article/116623 sexual
    -assault-patrick-henry-college-gods-harvard.
Fingerhut, Hannah. "Republicans Skeptical of Colleges' Impact on U.S., But
    Most See Benefits for Workforce Preparation." Pew Research Center, July
    20, 2017. https://www.pewresearch.org/fact-tank/2017/07/20/republicans-
    skeptical-of-colleges-impact-on-u-s-but-most-see-benefits-for-workforce-
    preparation/.
Folks, Titus, ed. *The Enduring Legacy of the Civil War.* Vimeo, 2013. https://vi-
    meo.com/110217438. Short film.
Frank, Adam. *The Constant Fire: Beyond the Science vs. Religion Debate.*
    Berkeley: University of California Press, 2009.
Galston, William A. "Has Trump Caused White Evangelicals to Change
    Their Tune on Morality?" Brookings.edu, October 19, 2016. https://www
    .brookings.edu/blog/fixgov/2016/10/19/has-trump-caused-white
    -evangelicals-to-change-their-tune-on-morality/.
George, Robert P. *Conscience and Its Enemies: Confronting the Dogmas of Liberal Secularism.* Wilmington, DE: ISI Books, 2016.
Ginsberg, Allen. "Howl." Poetry Foundation, accessed May 2, 2019. Originally
    published 1956. https://www.poetryfoundation.org/poems/49303/howl.
Goodman, William R., Jr., and James J. H. Price. *Jerry Falwell: An Unauthorized Profile.* Lynchburg, VA: Paris & Associates, 1981.
Griffith, R. Marie. *Moral Combat: How Sex Divided American Christians and
    Fractured American Politics.* New York: Hachette Book Group, 2017.
Guinness, Os. "Schaeffer's 'True Truth.'" Round Church Talks, May 15, 2014.
    https://www.christianheritage.org.uk/Media/AllMedia.aspx.
Haidt, Jonathan. *Righteous Mind: Why Good People Are Divided by Politics and
    Religion.* New York: Pantheon, 2012.
Harding, Susan Friend. *The Book of Jerry Falwell: Fundamentalist Language
    and Politics.* Princeton, NJ: Princeton University Press, 2000.
Hartley, Hal, dir. *Henry Fool.* Shooting Gallery and True Fiction Pictures.
    1997. Film.
Haught, Nancy. "William Hamilton, God-Is-Dead Theologian, Dies in Portland at 87." Oregonlive.com, February 29, 2012. http://blog.oregonlive.
    com/lifestories/2012/02/william_hamilton_god-is-dead_t.html.
Heidegger, Martin. *Nietzsche.* New York: HarperCollins, 1991.
"Highest-Paid Chief Executives at Private Nonprofit Colleges, 2014." *Chronicle
    of Higher Education,* August 13, 2017. https://www.chronicle.com/article/
    Highest-Paid-Chief-Executives/240489.

Hochschild, Arlie Russell. *Strangers in Their Own Land*. New York: New Press, 2016.

Hughes, Merrit Y., ed. *John Milton: Complete Poems and Major Prose*. New York: Prentice Hall, 1957.

Hutson, Matthew. "Are You Looking at Me?" *Aeon*, November 13, 2013. https://aeon.co/essays/what-goes-on-in-our-minds-when-we-see-someone -naked.

"Is God Dead." *Time*, April 8, 1966.

IPPNW Germany. "Body Count." Physicians for Social Responsibility, March 19, 2015. https://www.psr.org/blog/resource/body-count/.

John, Elton, vocalist. "Levon." By Elton John and Bernie Taupin. Recorded February 27, 1971. In *Madman across the Water*. Released by DJM and Uni Records. Record album.

Kaufmann, Walter, ed. *Existentialism from Dostoevsky to Sartre*. Cleveland: World Publishing, 1956.

———. *Religion from Tolstoy to Camus*. New York: Harper & Row, 1961.

Kelly, David. "The Earth Is Round, and Other Myths, Debunked by the Flat Earth Movement (You Read That Right). *Los Angeles Times*, January 15, 2018. https://www.latimes.com/nation/la-na-colorado-flat-earth-20180115- story.html.

Kierkegaard, Søren. *Kierkegaard: Letters and Documents*. Princeton, NJ: Princeton University Press. 1979.

———. *Purity of Heart Is to Will One Thing*. New York: Harper & Brothers, 1938.

Kilgore, Adam. "Liberty's Hiring of Ex-Baylor AD Sends a Chilling Message about Sexual Assault." *Washington Post*, November 29, 2016. https://www.washingtonpost.com/news/sports/wp/2016/11/29/ in-hiring-ian-mccaw-liberty-university-sends-a-chilling-message/.

Kreighbaum, Andrew. "Justice Department Will Back Suit on 'Free Speech' Zone." *Inside Higher Ed*, September 27, 2017. https://www.insidehighered .com/news/2017/09/27/attorney-general-sessions-blasts-colleges-issues -free-speech.

Kruse, Kevin M. *One Nation under God: How Corporate America Invented Christian America*. New York: Basic Books, 2015.

LaHaye, Tim. *How to Be Happy Though Married*. Wheaton, IL: Tyndale, 2002.

———. *The Unhappy Gays: What Everyone Should Know about Homosexuality*. Wheaton, IL: Tyndale, 1978.

LaHaye, Tim, and Beverly LaHaye. *The Act of Marriage: The Beauty of Sexual Love*. Grand Rapids, MI: Zondervan, 1998.

Leonhardt, David, and Stuart A. Thompson. "Trump's Lies." *New York Times*, December 14, 2017. https://www.nytimes.com/interactive/2017/06/23/ opinion/trumps-lies.html.

Lewis, Lisa. "Active Shooter Drills Normalize Atrocities." *Los Angeles Times*, December 8, 2015. https://www.latimes.com/opinion/op-ed/la-oe-1208- lewis-redlands-san-bernardino-lockdown-20151208-story.html.

Lienesch, Michael. *Redeeming America: Piety and Politics in the New Christian*

Right. Chapel Hill: University of North Carolina Press, 1993.

Lindsey, Hal. *The Late Great Planet Earth*. Grand Rapids, MI: Zondervan, 1970.

Lively, Scott. "An Open Letter to President Vladimir Putin." Scott Lively Ministries, August 30, 2013. http://www.scottlively.net/2013/08/30/an-open-letter-to-president-vladimir-putin/.

——. *The Pink Swastika: Homosexuality in the Nazi Party*. 5th ed. Sacramento: Veritas Aeterna Press, 2002.

Marklein, Mary Beth. "Jerry Falwell's Legacy: A Thriving Liberty University." *USA Today*, September 14, 2013. https://www.usatoday.com/story/news/nation/2013/09/14/liberty-university/2764789/.

Marsden, George M. *Fundamentalism and American Culture*. New York: Oxford University Press, 2006.

Mattison, Alice. "Where Do You Get Your Ideas?" *Writer's Chronicle* (February 2012): 52–64.

Mazza, Ed. "Mississippi Bill Would Let Churches Create Armed Security Squads." Huffpost, May 30, 2016. https://www.huffpost.com/entry/mississippi-church-gun-law_n_56fb4361e4b0a06d58040696.

McNear, Claire. "The Baylor Scandal Is Bigger Than Art Briles." *The Ringer*, February 3, 2017. https://www.theringer.com/2017/2/3/16044420/baylor-bears-football-program-art-briles-court-filing-2fc2103c5bb5.

Miller, Emily McFarlan. "Conservatives Defend Roy Moore—Invoking Joseph, Mary and the Ten Commandments." Religion News Service, November 10, 2017. https://religionnews.com/2017/11/10/conservatives-defend-roy-moore-invoking-joseph-mary-and-the-ten-commandments/.

Miller, Stephen P. *The Age of Evangelicalism: America's Born-Again Years*. New York: Oxford University Press, 2014.

Mitchell, Tony, Crispin Reece, and Christopher Spencer, dirs. *The Bible*. Aired March 3–31, 2013, on History Channel. LightWorkers Media. TV miniseries.

Myre, Greg. "A Tally of Mass Shootings in the U.S." NPR, December 3, 2015. https://www.npr.org/sectionsthetwo-way/2015/12/03/458321777/a-tally-of-mass-shootings-in-the-u-s.

Newport, Frank. "In U.S., 42% Believe in Creationist View of Human Origins." Gallup, June 2, 2014. https://news.gallup.com/poll/170822/believe-creationist-view-human-origins.aspx.

O'Connor, Flannery. *Wise Blood*. New York: Farrar, Straus & Giroux, 1949.

Oppel, Richard A., Jr., Sheryl Gay Stolberg, and Matt Apuzzo. "Justice Department to Release Blistering Report of Racial Bias by Baltimore Police." *New York Times*, August 9, 2016. https://www.nytimes.com/2016/08/10/us/justice-department-to-release-blistering-report-of-racial-bias-by-baltimore-police.html.

Parry, Robert. "The GOP's Own Asian Connection: Rev. Moon." *Los Angeles Times*, November 16, 1997. https://www.latimes.com/archives/la-xpm-1997-nov-16-op-54375-story.html.

Pashman, Manya Brachear. "Wheaton College Seeks to Fire Christian

Professor over View of Islam." *Chicago Tribune*, January 6, 2016. https://
www.chicagotribune.com/news/local/breaking/ct-wheaton-college-
professor-fired-20160105-story.html.

Peikoff, Leonard. *Objectivism: The Philosophy of Ayn Rand*. New York: Penguin Books, 1991.

Pence, Mike. "Mike Pence Believes in Biblical Creation." C-SPAN,
July 11, 2002. https://www.c-span.org/video/?c4631055/
mike-pence-believes-biblical-creation.

Pennington, Bill. "In Virginia's Hills, a Football Crusade." *New York Times*,
November 10, 2012.

Pérez-Peña, Richard. "Bob Jones University Blamed Victims of Sexual As-
saults, Not Abusers, Report Says." *New York Times*, December 11, 2014.
https://www.nytimes.com/2014/12/12/us/bob-jones-university-sex-assault-
victim-study.html.

———. "Christian School Faulted for Halting Abuse Study." *New York Times*,
February 11, 2014. https://www.nytimes.com/2014/02/12/education/
christian-school-faulted-for-halting-abuse-study.html.

Posner, Michael. "Ruling to Dismiss Federal Suit against Scott Lively."
SCRBD, June 5, 2017. https://www.scribd.com/document/350534580/
Ruling-to-dismiss-federal-suit-against-Scott-Lively#from_embed?-
campaign=SkimbitLtd&ad_group=126006X1587340X46cd52f45c-
c5f036e00d4464e937dd83&keyword=660149026&source=hp_affiliate&-
medium=affiliate.

Postman, Neil. 1985. *Amusing Ourselves to Death: Public Discourse in the Age
of Show Business*. 25th anniversary ed. New York: Penguin, 2006.

Pound, Ezra. "The Garden." Poetry Archive, accessed May 8, 2019. Originally
published 1916. https://www.poetry-archive.com/p/the_garden.html.

Prabhupada, A. C. Bhaktivedanta Swami. *Bhagavad-Gita As It Is*. Los Angeles: Bhaktivedanta Book Trust, 1972.

Prickett, Stephen. *Narrative, Religion and Science: Fundamentalism versus
Irony, 1700–1999*. Cambridge: Cambridge University Press, 2002.

Remarque, Erich Maria. *All Quiet on the Western Front*. New York: Ballantine
Books, 1982. Originally published 1929.

Roberts, David. "Donald Trump and the Rise of Tribal Epistemology."
Vox, May 19, 2017. https://www.vox.com/
policy-and-politics/2017/3/22/14762030/donald-trump-tribal-epistemology.

Robin, William. "Colin Kaepernick and the Radical Uses of 'The Star-
Spangled Banner.'" *New Yorker*, August 29, 2016.

Robinson, Marilynne. "Fear." *New York Review of Books*, September 24, 2015.
https://www.nybooks.com/articles/2015/09/24/marilynne-robinson-fear/.

Robinson, Marilynne, and Marcelo Gleiser. "Marilynne Robinson + Marcelo Gleiser, The Mystery We Are." *On Being with
Krista Tippett*, January 8, 2012. https://onbeing.org/programs/
marilynne-robinson-marcelo-gleiser-the-mystery-we-are/.

Robles, Frances, and Jim Rutenberg. "The Evangelical, the 'Pool Boy,' the

Comedian and Michael Cohen." *New York Times*, June 18, 2019. https://www.nytimes.com/2019/06/18/us/trump-falwell-endorsement-michael-cohen.html.

Rotondaro, Vinnie. "Disastrous Doctrine Had Papal Roots." *National Catholic Reporter*, September 4, 2015. https://www.ncronline.org/news/justice/disastrous-doctrine-had-papal-roots.

Russell, Bertrand. *The History of Western Philosophy*. New York: Simon & Schuster, 1945.

Scanlon, Kate. "Jerry Falwell Jr. Claims 'Establishment Republicans' Intentionally Leaked Lewd Trump Tape." *The Blaze*, October 10, 2016. https://www.theblaze.com/news/2016/10/10/jerry-falwell-jr-claims-establishment-republicans-intentionally-leaked-lewd-trump-tape.

Schaeffer, Francis A. *A Christian Manifesto*. Wheaton, IL: Crossway Books, 1981.

———. *Escape from Reason*. Downers Grove, IL: Intervarsity Press, 2006.

Self, Robert O. *All in The Family: The Realignment of American Democracy since the 1960s*. New York: Hill & Wang, 2012.

Sieczkowski, Cavan. "Samuel L. Jackson on Newtown School Shooting: Don't Blame Gun Control or Violence in Movies." Huffpost, December 18, 2012. https://www.huffpost.com/entry/samuel-l-jackson-newtown-school-shooting-gun-control-violence-in-movies_n_2321545.

Silverbush, Lori, and Kristi Jacobson, dirs. *A Place at the Table*. Motto Pictures and Participant Media. 2012. Film.

Simpson, Ian. "Evangelical Jerry Falwell Jr. to Head Trump Education Task Force." Reuters, February 1, 2017. https://www.reuters.com/article/us-usa-trump-falwell/evangelical-jerry-falwell-jr-to-head-trump-education-task-force-idUSKBN15G5F4.

Smietana, Bob. "New Research: Americans Believe in Heaven, Hell, and a Little Bit of Heresy." Lifeway Research, October 28, 2014. https://blog.lifeway.com/newsroom/2014/10/28/new-research-americans-believe-in-heaven-hell-and-a-little-bit-of-heresy/.

Smillie, Dirk. *Falwell Inc.: Inside a Religious, Educational, Political, and Business Empire*. New York: St. Martin's Press, 2008.

Solnit, Rebecca. "Cassandra among the Creeps." *Harper's Magazine*, October 2014.

Southern Poverty Law Center. "Extremist Files: Charles Murray." Accessed May 6, 2019. https://www.splcenter.org/fighting-hate/extremist-files/individual/charles-murray.

———. "Hate Map by Ideology." Accessed May 6, 2019. https://www.splcenter.org/hate-map/by-ideology.

Spencer, Christopher, dir. *Son of God*. Hearst Entertainment Productions and LightWorkers Media. 2014. Film.

Stanley, Charles. *A Man's Touch: Stepping into the Shoes Only a Dad Can Fill*. New York: Victor Books, 1992.

Stanton, Glenn. "How We Dishonor God in Our Sex Lives." Focus on the

Family, accessed May 8, 2019. https://www.focusonthefamily.com/marriage/sex-and-intimacy/gods-design-for-sex/how-we-dishonor-god-in-our-sex-lives. Reprinted from Glenn T. Stanton, *My Crazy Imperfect Christian Family* (Carol Stream, IL: NavPress, 2004).

Stenholm, Katherine, dir. *Sheffey*. Bob Jones University and Unusual Films. 1977. Film.

Sutton, Matthew Avery. *American Apocalypse: A History of Modern Evangelicalism*. Cambridge, MA: Belknap Press of Harvard University Press, 2014.

Symphony of Science. "A Wave of Reason." November 22, 2010. https://www.symphonyofscience.com/videos. Music video.

They Might Be Giants. *Here Comes Science*. John Flansburgh and John Linnell, vocalists. Disney Sound. Released July 1, 2009. Album.

Trent, Amy. "Trump Talks Tough at Liberty University." *News & Advance*, September 24, 2012. https://www.newsadvance.com/news/local/trump-talks-tough-at-liberty-university/article_43b796a0-4416-593d-bfc2-a942732c3722.html.

"Trump Dismisses Accusers as Women." *The Onion*, December 12, 2017. https://politics.theonion.com/trump-dismisses-accusers-as-women-1821226091.

Tyree, Elizabeth, and Caren Pinto. "Va. Sheriff Puts Up Billboard in Response to Kneeling Debate." *WSET ABC 13 News*, October 13, 2017. https://wset.com/news/local/bedford-co-sheriff-puts-up-billboard-in-response-to-kneeling-debate.

Unamuno, Miguel de. *Tragic Sense of Life*. New York: Dover Publications, 1954.

Vitello, Paul. "William Hamilton Dies at 87; Known for 'Death of God.'" *New York Times*, March 10, 2012. https://www.nytimes.com/2012/03/11/us/william-hamilton-known-for-death-of-god-idea-dies-at-87.html.

Volf, Miroslav. *Exclusion and Embrace: A Theological Exploration of Identity, Otherness, and Reconciliation*. Nashville, TN: Abingdon, 1996.

Westphal, Merold. *God, Guilt, and Death: An Existential Phenomenology of Religion*. Bloomington: Indiana University Press, 1984. Paperback reprint, 1987.

Willingham, A. J. "The Unexpected Connection between Slavery, NFL Protests and the National Anthem." CNN, August 22, 2017. https://www.cnn.com/2016/08/29/sport/colin-kaepernick-flag-protest-has-history-trnd/index.html.

Winant, Scott, dir. *Carnivàle*. Season 2, episode 12, "New Canaan, CA." Aired March 27, 2005, on Home Box Office. TV series.

Wong, Curtis M. "Homosexuality Is 'Unique from Any Other Sin' and an 'Attack on God,' Mat Staver Claims." Huffpost, July 9, 2014. https://www.huffpost.com/entry/homosexuality-mat-staver_n_5571849.

Woodruff, Betsy. "Inside Virginia's Creepy White-Power Wolf Cult." *Daily Beast*, November 12, 2015. https://www.thedailybeast.com/inside-virginias-creepy-white-power-wolf-cult.

Worthen, Molly. *Apostles of Reason: The Crisis of Authority in American Evangelicalism*. New York: Oxford University Press, 2014.

Wright, Richard. *Black Boy*. New York: HarperCollins, 1945.

X, Malcolm, as told to Alex Haley. *The Autobiography of Malcolm X*. New York: Ballantine Publishing Group, 1964.

Young, Neil J. *We Gather Together: The Religious Right and the Problem of Interfaith Politics*. New York: Oxford University Press, 2016.